KU-257-130

Gordon Batho

Political Issues
in Education

CASSELL

Cassell Educational Limited
Artillery House
Artillery Row
London SW1P 1RT

Copyright © Gordon Batho 1989

All rights reserved. No part of this publication may be reproduced or transmitted in any form or by any means, electronic or mechanical, including photocopying, recording or any information storage or retrieval system, without prior permission in writing from the publisher.

First published 1989

ISBN 0-304-31821-3 (hardback)
     0-304-31823-X (paperback)

Typeset by Activity Ltd, Salisbury, Wiltshire
Printed and bound in Great Britain by
Biddles Ltd, Guildford and King's Lynn

Contents

Foreword: The Purpose of This Series

The educational scene is changing rapidly. This change is being caused by a complexity of factors which includes a re-examination of present educational provision against a background of changing social and economic policies, the 1988 Education Reform Act, new forms of testing and assessment, a National Curriculum, local management of schools with more participation by parents.

As the educational process is concerned with every aspect of our lives and our society both now and for the future, it is of vital importance that all teachers, teachers in training, administrators and educational policy-makers should be aware and informed on current issues in education.

This series of books is thus designed to inform on current issues, look at emerging ones, and to give an authoritative overview which will be of immense help to all those involved in the education process.

Political Issues in Education, by Professor Gordon Batho of the University of Durham, begins the series by looking at the development of education in terms of four ages — expansion, consensus, politicization and, currently, centralization. It is therefore of key importance to the series as it sets education in its historical and political context.

Philip Hills
Cambridge
September 1989

Introduction

This book is an introduction to the history of education in England and Wales which will be of value to the general reader as well as to teacher trainees. The history of education is often dismissed as irrelevant, not only by the public at large, but even by professional teachers, educational administrators and teacher trainers. This is despite the total revolution in the study which has occurred in the last twenty years or so. At one time, admittedly, the history of education was essentially preoccupied with the histories of formalized educational institutions, with the development of educational ideas and theories, and with the details of educational legislation. This is no longer the case. Nowadays it is seen as a subject which utilizes the advances in methodology of history itself, which draws on the techniques of the social sciences, and which sets the evolution of education (not just schooling) in the context of international as well as national and regional factors, political and religious issues, social and economic circumstances, psychological and philosophical considerations.

Far from being irrelevant, the history of education is a radical study. The professional ignores it at his peril, the amateur to his disadvantage. For it teaches that things have not always been as they now are and can therefore be changed. The history of education also teaches that the 'new' is as often as not the 'old' in new clothing, that the issues in education are mostly enduring and the solutions proposed have generally been tried before in some form or other. There is the great advantage that the debates of a past generation can be considered dispassionately. The era of the School Boards, established under the 1870 Act to 'fill the gaps' of voluntary provision and abolished under the 1902 Act in favour of local authorities, very well illustrates the point. Attendance was a major problem, for example, when attendance officers (or 'the School Board men' as they were known colloquially long after 1902) were first appointed. Attendance remained a live issue in many parts of the country in the 1920s and 1930s. Unfortunately, attendance is again giving rise to real concern at the present time; in autumn 1988 it was reported that perhaps as many as 7,000 children are running loose on school afternoons in the centre of England's second city, Birmingham. The coercion of the unwilling to go to school is still necessary more than a hundred years after the establishment of a national system of elementary education. The history of education also teaches that local agencies can be more effective in some educational endeavours than central government. It was the locally elected School Boards which in the 1880s outran the central authority (and their own powers as it happens) in providing a widened curriculum in the higher grade schools, in some ways forerunners of our modern-day sixth form colleges. We talk of parent power and point both to the provision in the 1944 Act that, as far as may be feasible, children should be taught in accordance with parents' wishes and to the recent requirements for the appointment of parent governors. We would do well to remember that the absence of a property qualification for election to School Boards led to extensive parent representation on many of them — and working-class parents at that. Or again the Assisted Places Scheme of the 1980s was presaged by the power of School Boards to pay the fees of pupils at voluntary schools if they deemed it appropriate.

The history of education also teaches that economic expediency has frequently been as powerful a consideration in educational reform as any educational philosophy and that administration, including the personal predilections of a senior administrator, can be more determinant than legislation in practice. There is the story, well-known to historians of education, of the discoveries of the newly appointed headmaster of 'Fircroft Comprehensive School'. He asked the caretaker to remove the noticeboard above the front door of his solidly built late-nineteenth-century school. The noticeboard read 'Fircroft Secondary Modern School'. On the back, the words 'Fircroft Senior School' were painted neatly, but etched deeply into the stone lintel were found the words 'Fircroft Board School'. The story is apocryphal but the point is real enough: sometimes educational advance has been not much more than a change of name. We are currently debating the introduction of the National Curriculum. Indeed, some observers have felt that we are in danger of being obsessed with the National Curriculum and with the tests which are to accompany its adoption. Certainly, the history of education teaches that it is very much easier to test quantitative than qualitative learning, though, as Sir Alec Clegg, the chief education officer for the West Riding, reminded us, it is the qualitative learning that really matters. But how many appreciate that the National Curriculum bears a marked (perhaps alarming?) resemblance to the Board of Education Regulations of 1904, written by Robert Morant, an official of the Board, deliberately to exclude the commercial and industrial aspects from the secondary school curriculum?

This book may stimulate discussion of where the responsibility for the development of educational provision in this country has lain and where the control of education should properly lie in the future. It is meant to be evocative and provocative rather than authoritative, though it is hoped that it will be accepted, like the National Curriculum, as balanced and relevant.

1 Educational development in an age of expansion, 1833–1944

Introduction

> We recognise now that book-learning, by itself, fails to afford any adequate mental training ... The student or pupil ... must be trained in methods of discovery ... The teacher's functions are consequently widened. He has to stimulate in his pupils activity of thought, and must not assume that it is there. (Magnus, 1910, p. 138)

These words were written, not of the General Certificate of Secondary Education in 1988, but of the examinations of the City and Guilds of London Institute in 1910 by the Institute's first secretary, Sir Philip Magnus. They are a reminder of the continuity of thinking in education which has been as potent in the development of English schooling as the capacity for change.

Elementary education 1833–59

Historically, of course, the provision of education was the prerogative of the Church. The two most influential agencies of education, however rudimentary, for the ordinary people of Britain around 1800 were both closely associated with the Church — the Charity Schools and the Sunday Schools. In 1833 the first central government funds were made available for the elementary education of the general public in the form of £20,000 of building aid for two voluntary societies — the National Society (for Promoting the Education of the Poor in the Principles of the Established Church) and the British and Foreign School Society. These had been founded in the 1810s to further

1

the work initiated by the Reverend Andrew Bell and Joseph Lancaster respectively in establishing the cost-effective monitorial scheme of teaching. It was not until 1839 that a central government body concerned with education was created: the Committee of the Privy Council on Education, which proceeded to monitor the grants to schools and to appoint Her Majesty's Inspectors to report on conditions in the localities — to act, in fact, as the eyes and ears of the central government. The secretary to the Committee, Dr James Kay-Shuttleworth, was clear that his duty was to assert the claims of the civil power to control the education of the country. But this was not a general view. Henry Brougham, the Lord Chancellor, had been one of the most ardent advocates of popular education but his evidence to the Parliamentary Committee on the State of Education in 1834 was opposed to State provision:

> Do you think that a system of primary education, established by law, would be beneficial? I think that it is wholly inapplicable to the present condition of the country, and the actual state of education. Those who recommend it on account of its successful adoption on the Continent, do not reflect upon the funds which it would require, and upon the exertions already made in this country by individual beneficence.
>
> (*Report of the Parliamentary Committee*, 1834, p. 220)

The Factory Act of 1833 limited the employment of children between the ages of 9 and 12 to eight hours a day and between 13 and 18 to twelve hours. It applied to all textile factories except silk mills. More significantly, it laid down that children under 13 were to receive two hours' schooling on six days a week. Four government inspectors were appointed to enforce the Act but, true to the English tradition of amateurism, the Act made no provision for their training. The half-time system, as it came to be called, lasted until 1918, and was the earliest attempt to impose education by law.

Teachers were themselves untrained until the Church began to establish diocesan colleges from 1839 and Kay-Shuttleworth introduced a pupil-teacher system for students aged 13 to 18 from 1846. By now, the deficiencies of the monitorial system were widely recognized. In the words of HMI F.C. Cook:

> We cannot reflect upon the age or requirements of monitors without being struck with the absurdity of expecting any good results from the use of such materials. Taking the average age of monitors, they may be described as boys about eleven and a half years old, reading with ease, but not much intelligence; writing from dictation, so as to give the sense of a passage, but without any regard to punctuation, or any practical knowledge of grammar; with more or less facility in working the ordinary rules of arithmetic to proportion or practice, but with little or no insight into its principles. The knowledge of geography, history or general information, which the more intelligent of these youths may possess, is not called for in their employment … and it is hardly needful here to reiterate the severe but just observations which all writers upon our National Schools have made upon the tone and character of the religious instruction under monitors.
>
> (*Report of the Committee of Council on Education*, 1845, I, pp. 163–4)

Teacher training in the diocesan colleges was often irrelevant, for the staff were almost exclusively Oxbridge graduates, usually in orders, certainly without experience of elementary education, and extraordinarily limited in scope and vision. In the words of the Reverend Derwent Coleridge, first principal of St Mark's College, Chelsea:

> The object being to produce schoolmasters for the poor, the endeavour must be on the one hand to raise the students morally and intellectually to a certain standard, while, on the other hand, we train them in lowly service.
>
> (*Report of the Committee of Council on Education*, 1842–3, p. 197)

Or as the Reverend H. Moseley, HMI, put it in 1846:

> We break off a fragment from the education we suppose necessary for our own children — its mechanical and technical part — and give it to the poor man's child in charity. The inveterate prejudice that education in any higher sense is a privilege annexed to a definite social position and graduated by it, associates itself with all our educational efforts. (Quoted in Rich, 1970, p. 9)

It was coming to be recognized that there was a case on economic and moral grounds for providing education at a basic level for all and the opportunity to go further for those who could. For example, Mr M.W. Willis, QC, MP for Colchester in 1839, in opening a Sunday school at Kelvedon, Essex, remarked:

> If you will only just give them reading, writing and arithmetic that is just enough to make them what you may call efficient as machines and implements and so long as they shall not venture to think for themselves they are content. For my part I would put no limit on the instruction that I would bestow upon a human being except the limit of my capacity to confer it and its capacity to receive it.
>
> (Essex Record Office D/MW24/3, quoted in P.J. Griffiths, London MA, 1984)

The dominating philosophy of the period was 'self-help', encapsulated in Samuel Smiles's book of that title in 1859. The social changes brought about by the Industrial Revolution not only concentrated large numbers of the population in a few areas and thus occasioned concern among the ruling classes for the socialization of the workers and of their children, they also encouraged among the working classes a genuine desire to read and for self-improvement. A popular literature emerged and up and down the country, in villages as well as in towns, corresponding and literary and philosophical (i.e., scientific) societies flourished which promoted reading and discussion among the more upwardly mobile working classes. Adults attended Sunday schools with their children or went to the adult schools established by nonconformist voluntary effort. Mechanics' institutes spread from Glasgow, where George Birkbeck had pioneered the concept in the 1820s, and provided opportunities for artisans to acquire some scientific learning. But often enough the paternalistic attitude taken towards the ordinary workers discouraged them from participation and led them to prefer to spend their evenings in the convivial atmosphere of one of the many public houses of nineteenth-century industrial cities — just as they were frequently prepared to pay small fees for their children to attend little schools run by one of their own class rather than to send them free to a voluntarily provided school. As Professor F.M.L. Thompson has argued, the working classes were astutely discriminating in their response to the various well-intended moves to educate and socialize them: 'rejecting the moral and controlling purposes by simply allowing the attempts at indoctrination in the ideology of submission to pass over their heads or run like water off a duck's back' (Thompson, 1981, p. 193).

Value for money

Despite all the efforts of the voluntary societies — and they were very considerable — the annual government grant had risen to over half a million pounds by 1857. As a consequence, a Royal Commission was appointed under the chairmanship of the Duke of Newcastle to enquire into the state of popular education and to advise on measures required for the extension of 'sound and cheap elementary education to all classes of people'. The Commission's enquiries led them to believe that most children were attending school at some time but that many teachers were ineffective and others failed to concentrate adequately on the basics. Children were often absent and too many left school too early:

> When it is remembered that agricultural wages range from 9s. to 14s. a week and that children can add to this sum sometimes as much as 4s. or 5s. and generally 2s. 6d., the importance of their earnings to their parents becomes sufficiently apparent.
>
> *(Report*, 1861, vol. VII, 1, p. 182)

Attendance was to be the major problem in education until after the First World War. The Reverend F. Watkins, HMI, had reported in 1846 that of the 495 teachers whom he had met in grant-earning schools in the north of England in the previous year, one-third were 'neither intended by nature nor fitted by art for the situation in which they are placed' (Minutes of Council, 1845, xxxii, p. 298). Dr W.B. Hodgson put matters more colourfully to the Newcastle Commission:

> None are too old, too poor, too ignorant, too feeble, too sickly, too

unqualified in any or every way to regard themselves, and to be regarded by others, as unfit for schoolkeeping. Nay, there are few, if any occupations regarded as incompatible with schoolkeeping, if not as simultaneous, at least as preparatory, employments.

> (*Report*, 1861, vol. III, p. 483)

To remedy this ineffective use of resources the Commissioners recommended:

> a searching examination by competent authority of every child in every school to which grants are paid with a view to ascertaining whether these indispensable elements of knowledge are thoroughly acquired and to make the prospects and positions of the teachers dependent to a considerable extent on the results of the examination.
>
> (*Report*, 1861, vol. VII, 1, p. 157)

Thus the 'payment by results' system — called by Harold Silver 'the most articulated version of educational accountability in English history' (Silver, 1980, p. 93) — came to be instituted in 1862. The Code was modified from time to time, as in 1875 when grants were made for class proficiency rather than individual attainment, and eventually abandoned in 1895, though the concept has been revived in a new form in the 1980s. The Revised Code, which came into force in 1862, helped to improve attendance, a much greater problem than the Commission appreciated, and led to a new and probably much needed concentration on the lower standards, as the classes were called in this period. It also involved trauma for the teachers and the children on the annual inspection day and for as much as a century soured the relationship between teachers and inspectors and those who were classed in a similar category, such as lecturers in education. This attitude is demonstrated in this story related by James Runciman in his *Schools and Scholars*:

> A brilliant young friend of mine was dying of consumption ... He was stretched out — frail and hectic, but cheerful and sweet as usual. Someone brought in a report that the inspector was dead: the dying man started up, a wild light struck out of his eyes, like fire from steel, and he said, with a hideous broken scream, 'By God, I hope he's in hell.' (Runciman, 1887, p. 264)

James Hall, a pupil at Elswick School near Newcastle upon Tyne from 1869 to 1871, gave a pupil's viewpoint:

> [The inspector] took the shape, in our young minds, of the fiend incarnate, the theological Satan becoming dethroned ... when the dreaded day came our fears were dispelled, as he proved to be really milder and more human than some of our own teachers who, for weeks previously, had been in a state of strain and nervous irritation which more or less affected us. (Hall, 1912, p. 10)

Filling the gaps

The Elementary Education Act of 1870 was an ingenious compromise aimed at creating a public elementary educational system at least cost with least loss of voluntary help and greatest possible aid from the parents. In areas where the voluntary societies would not, or could not, supply the need for elementary education, a school board was to be established by local ratepayers with the power to levy an educational rate and to build schools as necessary. Additionally, the boards were to receive government grants. Attendance was not to be compulsory but the Act allowed school boards to make bye-laws for attendance between the ages of 5 and 13, with exemption from 10 to 13 if it was felt to be desirable. Schooling was not to be free; every child was to pay the fees prescribed by the school board but the fees were not to exceed ninepence a week. On the all-important religious issue, the government accepted an amendment (the Cowper–Temple clause) which laid down that in schools 'hereafter established by means of local rates, no catechism or religious formulary which is distinctive to any particular denomination shall be taught'. Voluntary schools received a 50 per cent grant from the government but building grants as such came to an end. In his speech introducing the Bill in the House of Commons, Mr W.E. Forster, the Vice-President of the Privy Council, declared its purpose to be 'to bring elementary education within the reach of every English home, aye, and within the reach of those children who have no homes' (Maclure, 1971, p. 104).

The Bill pleased none of the pressure groups and was passed amidst bitter controversy. In retrospect, it has been seen as 'the first piece of modern social legislation, full of innovations, from the adoption of a secret ballot in elections (of school boards) to the introduction of substantial delegated legislation' (Middleton, 1976, p. 57).

The Act, and subsequent nineteenth-century legislation, such as Mundella's Act making elementary education compulsory throughout the country (1880) and the Act abolishing fees in provided elementary schools (1891), achieved in thirty years a national system of elementary education and made it normal for children to attend school. The urban school boards were especially successful and from the mid-1870s many supported 'higher grade schools' to give the opportunity for a more advanced education to those prepared to stay at school. As early as 1879 some opposed what they saw as a second-rate secondary education, as this comment in the *Sheffield Telegraph* demonstrates:

> They offer a middle-class education at half the prime cost of the commodity to be supplied — they compete destructively with useful and honoured institutions which are based on honesty to pay their way without help from the rates. (Armytage, 1951, p. 217)

The 2,500 boards which developed varied greatly in size and quality, from those having three members and one small, rural school to those having fifteen members and a range of schools serving populations exceeding 100,000. The board schools had an advantage over the voluntary from their access to the rates (though until the early twentieth century voluntary schools provided more school places: in 1895 2,400,000 as against 1,900,000), but found difficulty in providing an adequate supply of trained teachers, so that the Education Department was obliged to use 'Article 68' women teachers. The 1890 Code for Elementary Schools provided in article 68 for the use

> in mixed, girls, and infant schools, [of] a woman over 18 years of age, approved by the Inspector, who is employed during the whole of the school hours in the general instruction of the scholars and is

recognised as an additional female teacher.

— that is, provided she had been vaccinated! As the Reverend F. Stone testified of his board school education at Medburn Street, London, in the late 1880s:

> We were taught to write clearly, to spell correctly — which cannot be said of modern education — to know the great passages of the Bible and to have an elementary knowledge of history and geography.
>
> (*Times Educational Supplement*, 23 December 1966)

By 1900 the Registrar-General could report a literacy rate for men and women of around 97 per cent, whereas in 1871 it had been 80 and 73 per cent respectively. It was a remarkable achievement.

Secondary and higher education in the later nineteenth century

No direct financial support for secondary or university education was provided before 1889, apart from Science and Art grants consequent upon the success of the 1851 Exhibition, but the central government redistributed large amounts of money in the middle decades of the century. This money came from the endowments of grammar and public schools and of the ancient universities of Oxford and Cambridge.

In 1850 Lord Russell appointed a Royal Commission to enquire into the State, Discipline, Studies and Revenues of Oxford and Cambridge. Its recommendations led to major changes in curricula and customs: new provision for the teaching of science, the abolition of religious tests in 1871, the introduction of examinations taken by boys (and girls) from the grammar and public schools, the establishment of new chairs and the reform of fellowships, which was perhaps the most important change of all. Unless this were the reform which permitted the creation of women's colleges at the ancient universities (although in fact women were not admitted to degrees at Cambridge, for example, until 1948). Private enterprise and civic concern led to the establishment of new universities — London from 1828

9

onwards, Durham from 1832, and then the 'civic' universities from 1851 — Manchester leading the way.

The 1860s saw the appointment of Royal Commissions on the public schools (the Clarendon Commission 1861–4) and on the endowed schools (the Taunton Commission 1864–7). The Clarendon Commission advocated a widening of the public school curriculum and a restructuring of governing bodies, a matter dealt with by the Public Schools Act of 1868, but praised the achievements of the schools in producing English gentlemen:

> It is not easy to estimate the degree in which the English people are indebted to these schools for the qualities on which they pique themselves most — for their capacity to govern others and control themselves, their aptitude for combining freedom with order, their public spirit, their vigour and manliness of character, their strong but not slavish respect for public opinion, their love of healthy sports and exercise. (*Report*, 1864, p. 56)

The schools not included in the Reports of the Clarendon or Newcastle Commissions were the subject of scrutiny by the Schools Inquiry Commission under Lord Taunton, probably the most far-reaching survey of English educational history. It considered 782 endowed schools, 122 proprietary and a number of private schools, girls' education as well as boys', and took evidence from America and Europe as well as from this country. A year after the publication of the Report, the Endowed Schools Act ignored most of the Commission's recommendations but appointed three Commissioners to recognize the charitable trusts belonging to the endowed schools and increased the number of endowments for the education of girls significantly from twelve in the 1860s to eighty in the 1890s. The Act presaged the concept of an 'educational ladder'. The Commission's proposals for a national system of secondary schools, graded by the age of leaving (14, 16 or 18), were not accepted.

By 1895, when the Bryce Commission was appointed to report on secondary education, two-thirds of the 1,448 grammar schools in England had been reformed and secondary education for girls had been extended very considerably, yet the Bryce

Commission found that scholarships to secondary schools were inadequate. Meanwhile the Department of Science and Art was offering grants for the teaching of science, which many grammar schools took up. By the Technical Instruction Act of 1889 the county and county borough councils established by the Local Government Act of 1888 were empowered (but not required) to levy a penny rate to aid technical instruction and under the Local Taxation (Customs and Excise) Act of 1890 part of the customs revenue was made available to support the extension of technical education. In 1899, at last the Board of Education was established as a central authority for education, as urged by the Taunton and Bryce Reports. It absorbed the work of the Science and Art and the Education Departments. The 1899 Act also provided for the formation of a Consultative Committee, which was to produce influential reports on education in the twentieth century.

The Education Act of 1902

Education, being a social activity, cannot avoid reflecting the social relationships of society. By 1900, after half a century of promoting and of provision by central government and initiatives taken by local agencies, whether charities or publicly constituted bodies, England still did not have a real system for universal education but it did have a structure which mirrored the perceived needs of various classes. There were elementary schools for the lower working classes, higher grade and technical schools for the more ambitious, endowed grammar schools and public schools for the middle and upper classes. And there were distinctions made between the provision for the different strata of the middle classes. As Cecil Reddie, head of the progressive private foundation at Abbotsholme, put it in his evidence to the Bryce Commission, there should be schools for the muscle-worker, for the Briton 'whose work requires knowledge of the modern world' and for 'the Briton who is to be a leader'; with leaving ages of 14, 16 and 18 respectively. Reddie was merely echoing the ideas expressed earlier in the century by Canon Woodard and by the Taunton Commissioners.

11

In 1902 Robert Morant, who had worked in the Education Department since 1895, became Permanent Secretary to the Board of Education. He was responsible for drafting and implementing the Education Act which A.J. Balfour steered through Parliament that year. The Board had understandable difficulties in co-ordinating education when over 2,500 School Boards had to be dealt with individually and the demise of the Boards was finally heralded when Cockerton, auditor of the Local Government Board, decided that part of the expenditure of the London School Board was not on elementary education. The Act made county and county borough councils local education authorities 'to supply or aid the supply of education other than elementary, and to promote the general co-ordination of all forms of education' (Part II). Non-county boroughs with a population of over 10,000 and urban districts of over 20,000 were to be responsible for elementary education in their areas ('Part III authorities') so that the Board only had to regulate 318 local education authorities. Under the Act voluntary bodies were relieved of some financial burdens. While they were to continue to be responsible for providing and maintaining school buildings, local authorities were to make good any deficiencies brought about by fair wear and tear and the payment of teachers' salaries was to be from public funds. In rural areas it often happened that the Church of England village school was the only one in the district. Nonconformists saw this provision for the voluntary schools as 'Rome on the rates' and fierce resistance occurred to the Act, especially in Wales. The local authorities, now empowered to provide education other than elementary, established grammar schools, which did so much to promote social mobility in the early twentieth century, and training colleges, which established child-centredness as the essential feature of teacher training. As Sidney Webb put it in an article in the *Daily Mail* of 17 October 1902:

> For the first time the Bill definitely includes as a public function, education as education, not primary education only or technical education only, but anything and everything that is education from the kindergarten to the university.

The implementation of the 1902 Act

Morant set about restructuring education under the Act in his customary autocratic way. The Elementary School Code of 1904 declared the purpose of the elementary school:

> to form and strengthen the character and to develop the intelligence of the children entrusted to it, and to make the best of the school years available, in assisting both girls and boys, according to their different needs, to fit themselves, practically as well as intellectually, for the work of life.

The Regulations for Secondary Schools of the same year stressed the importance of a balanced curriculum; the scheme was based on the work of the public and endowed schools of the previous century but it has a curiously modern ring to it in 1989:

> The Course should provide for instruction in the English Language and Literature, at least one language other than English, geography, history, mathematics, science and drawing, with due provision for manual work and physical exercises, and, in a girls' school, for Housewifery. Not less than four and a half hours per week must be allotted to English, geography and history; not less than three and a half hours to the language where only one is taken or less than six hours where two are taken, and not less than seven and a half hours to science and mathematics, of which at least three must be for science. The instruction in science must be both theoretical and practical. When two languages other than English are taken, and Latin is not one of them, the Board will require to be satisfied that the omission of Latin is for the advantage of the school.

For the elementary school, by contrast, centralized control was replaced by the Board's *Handbook of Suggestions for the Consideration of Teachers*, first issued in 1905 and constantly revised until the Second World War. The liberality of approach is epitomized in the classic comment in the Prefatory Note:

> The only uniformity of practice that the Board of Education desire to see in the teaching of Public Elementary Schools is that each teacher shall think for himself, and work out for himself such methods of teaching as may use his powers to the best advantage and be best suited to the particular needs and conditions of the school.

13

In 1907 Supplementary Regulations for Secondary Schools established a scholarship system of 'free places' to allow able pupils from elementary schools to have a secondary education; such scholars were normally to occupy a quarter of the places in a secondary school. This was the origin of the 11-plus examination which, as the demand for secondary education increased, became very competitive.

Morant's predecessor, Sir George Kekewich, has recorded that when he became Secretary to the Education Department in 1890 he had two matters especially in mind in framing a new code of regulations for elementary schools:

> The first was to substitute for the bald teaching of facts and the cramming which was then necessary in order that the children might pass the annual examination… the development of interest and intelligence and the acquirement of real substantial knowledge. The second was the recognition, for the first time, of the duty of the State to care for the physical welfare of the children.
>
> (Kekewich, 1920, pp. 53–4)

Between 1890 and 1918 public attention was increasingly drawn to the problem of children's health. Mary Tabor in her contribution to Charles Booth's *Life and Labour of the People of London* in 1891 gave a graphic description of underfed children:

> Puny, pale-faced, scantily-clad and badly shod, those small and feeble folk may be found sitting limp and chill on the school benches in all the poorer parts of London. They swell the bills of mortality as want and sickness thin them off, or survive to be the needy and enfeebled adults whose burden of helplessness the next generation will have to fear. (Booth, 1902, vol. III, p. 207)

The Boer War exposed the poor physical condition of many volunteers. In 1906 an Education (Provision of Meals) Act allowed, but did not require, local authorities to provide school meals and in 1907 a further Act required local authorities to institute school medical examinations. The creation of a medical department of the Board of Education probably did more to promote educational advance than any education act.

Morant was removed from office in October 1911 as a result of the publication of an internal memorandum (the Holmes–Morant Circular) which characterized local authority inspectors 'as a rule uncultured and imperfectly educated' (Armytage, 1970, p. 203). He was succeeded by Lewis Selby-Bigge who held that control of education should be a partnership between the Board, local education authorities and teachers' associations. As he remained Permanent Secretary until 1925 he exercised a powerful influence in the development of effective consultation and consensus in educational matters.

The Education Act of 1918

Thanks to Selby-Bigge the Education Act of 1918 was a culmination to reform movements and proposals from the Boer to the Great War. The School Certificate Examination and a Secondary Schools Examination Council had both been instituted in 1917 to create order out of the previous chaos of proliferating public examinations and there had been an intention to strengthen central government's involvement in education by other measures, including the abolition of the 'Part III authorities'. In the event, the Act strengthened the local authorities, reformed the grant system so that not less than half the cost of education was funded centrally, abolished fees in elementary schools totally, removed all exemptions from the school-leaving age of 14 and enlarged the ancillary services the authorities were allowed to provide. It also, most significantly, proposed the creation of county colleges. As H.A.L. Fisher, the President of the Board of Education, explained to the Commons in introducing the Bill:

> I now come to the most novel if not the most important provision in the Bill. We propose that, with certain exceptions ... every young person no longer under any obligation to attend a public elementary school shall attend such continuation school as the local education authority ... may require for ... the equivalent of eight hours a week for forty weeks. (Quoted in Maclure, 1971, p. 174)

15

The Hadow Report on the Education of the Adolescent (1926)

The county colleges fell victim to the economic depression of the inter-war period but a number of real advances were made in the schools in what was in fact the heyday of local authority influence on education. The major differences of the period were, as R. Barker has written, 'over the speed and extent of reform, rather than over its direction' (Barker, 1972, p. 49). R.H. Tawney, the author of the Labour Party's policy document *Secondary Education for All* (1922), was a member of the Consultative Committee of the Board of Education which produced the Hadow Report on the Education of the Adolescent in 1926. The Report recommended the raising of the school-leaving age to 15, which did not in fact occur until after the Second World War. Importantly, it advocated the separation of primary from secondary education, a proposal which was not fully achieved for a whole historian's generation of thirty-three years but which made possible the evolution of a tripartite organization of secondary schools and enlarged the concept of secondary education beyond the kind of course given in grammar schools to 'modern secondary schools':

> regard being paid on the one hand to the requirements of a good general education and the desirability of providing a reasonable variety of curriculum ... for children of varying tastes and abilities, and on the other hand the probable occupations of the pupils in commerce, industry and agriculture. (Sullivan, 1980, p. 2)

The age of eleven was chosen as the dividing line between primary and secondary education on psychological advice: 'There is a tide which begins to rise in the veins of youth at the age of eleven or twelve. It is called by the name of adolescence' (Maclure, 1971, p. 180).

The Hadow Report on the Primary School (1931)

'The key word was economy, economy all the time,' remarked an ex-teacher to Cheryl Parsons when the latter was researching the history of Carbrook Church of England School (Sheffield) during the 1930s:

> economy that meant a shortage of the smaller things such as exercise books, sewing and art materials, as well as larger items such as adequate cupboard space or the prompt replacement of old worn-out desks and stock. (Parsons, 1978, pp. 123–4)

The economic depression halted school building, led to cuts in teachers' salaries in crises in 1922–3 and 1931, and made it difficult to implement the Hadow Report's most memorable recommendation: 'The curriculum is to be thought of in terms of activity and experience rather than of knowledge to be acquired and facts to be stored' (Maclure, 1971, p. 192). It is important, however, to note that a few pages later the Report comments: 'It would be unnecessary and pedantic to attempt to throw the whole of the teaching of the primary school into the project form.'

The Spens Report (1938)

After the Hadow Report of 1926 the Spens Report of 1938 was the most influential of the Consultative Committee's reports of the inter-war period. It covered the grammar schools and junior technical schools which were not included in the terms of reference of the first Hadow Report. The essence of its recommendations was that secondary education should continue to be developed in separate grammar, technical and modern schools. It 'reluctantly' rejected multi-lateral schools on the grounds that they would have to be large and therefore impersonal, that the sixth form would be proportionally too small, that it would be difficult to recruit suitable heads, and that they would be too expensive. The Report favoured experimentation and criticized the county grammar schools for imitating the public schools and for failing to develop quasi-vocational courses for pupils who wanted to enter industry or commerce at the age of 16. One of the more deplorable consequences of the

Depression had been the introduction of means testing for pupils who won 'special places' in secondary schools (Board of Education Circular 1421 of 1931) on the results of the 11-plus examination. Many grammar schools, however, admitted at small fees pupils who had failed the scholarship examination but whose parents wanted to have the kudos of a grammar school education. Many such pupils entered business at the age of 16. The statistics suggest that the number of pupils in secondary grammar schools in England and Wales rose from 337,000 in 1921 to 470,000 in 1938 but much of the increase is probably due to pupils staying on longer; the actual intake remained around 90,000 per annum (98,000 in 1938). By 1939 63.5 per cent of pupils over eleven were in reorganized schools but it must be remembered that only existing secondary schools came under the Board's Secondary Regulations. All the post-primary schools remained under the Elementary Code with its inferior levels of staffing, equipment and accommodation and larger class sizes.

University and adult education

The number of students attending universities in England, Wales and Scotland rose from 20,000 in 1900 to 50,000 in 1938 and charters were granted to Birmingham (1900), Liverpool (1903), Leeds (1904), Sheffield (1905), Bristol (1909) and Reading (1926). Public aid — £15,000 — was first given in 1889 and the University Grants Committee was established in 1919 to administer Treasury grants, which by then exceeded a million pounds. The scale of the country's higher education had, therefore, increased very markedly in the period though it was still a fairly modest exercise. At least the university colleges were freed from what many have seen as the narrowing influence of the local authorities:

> Once more in English administrative history, central authority and control have increased freedom and efficiency by interfering with local government. (Vaizey, 1963, pp. 172–3)

Just as significant an increase was seen in the involvement of universities in extension work. The Workers' Educational Association (WEA) founded in 1903, a dream-child of Albert Mansbridge, existed to involve ordinary working people in university-type studies and enlisted the enthusiastic support of university teachers, among them R.H. Tawney; of local authorities; of the co-operative societies; and of the established and the emergent universities. By 1939 the WEA had over 60,000 students.

In all the educational developments of the early twentieth century, however, it was the vocal middle class which benefited most. In the words of Ernest Cartwright, a railway-signalman from the Midlands who was a member of the WEA and an ardent self-improver:

> It is unfortunately too apparent to any observer that the working class do not value education as they ought to do. They regard it as a mere frill or embellishment of life that is not worth either the time, trouble or expense required in obtaining it. (Unpublished journal in University of Durham Education Library, vol. 23, p. 50)

It was an attitude which was to change, albeit slowly.

As Professor George Sampson put it in his *English for the English*:

> The national mind must be got to see that education is a spirit and not a substance. Education is not something of which we must acquire a certain quantity and can then be relieved for ever ... Education is a preparation for life, not merely for a livelihood, for living not for *a* living. (Sampson, 1926, pp. 3–4)

2 Educational development in an age of consensus, 1944–64

When R.A. Butler was moved from the Foreign Office to be President of the Board of Education in the summer of 1941, Winston Churchill, then Prime Minister, said to him: 'Tell the children that Wolfe won Quebec'. Butler replied that much as he would like to influence school curricula, it was frowned upon in England that the Minister should attempt to do so and Churchill responded: 'Of course not by instruction or order but by suggestion' (Butler, 1982, p. 90).

The exchange between Butler and Churchill epitomizes the tension which has always existed in educational politics from the time of the first state grant for education in 1833 — the tension between centralization and decentralization, the tension over what provision should be made for educating the young and, in particular, who should control what occurs in the classroom. It was to be Butler's greatest achievement to reconcile the conflicting forces in English society in the 1940s and to produce a legislative measure in the Education Act of 1944 which was agreed in Parliament and commanded virtually universal support among parents and teachers, bureaucrats and politicians. Butler was to say in 1943 that his Bill was really no more than 'codifying existing practice, which always seems to me to be the hallmark of good legislation' (Jeffereys, 1984, p. 430) and inevitably the Act incorporated a lot of thinking which had been undertaken between the wars.

But Butler richly deserved his success, for the Act was also the culmination of years of personal endeavour, of wide consultation and sensitive reaction to what the various groups involved in the education process put to him. In the words of a shrewd observer at the time, H.C. Dent: 'He first made himself master of the intricacies of the problem to a degree no previous statesman had done' (in Sullivan, 1980, p. vi). Butler was at pains in his memoirs to acknowledge the debt which he owed to his Parliamentary Secretary, Chuter Ede, and to his senior officials.

None the less, it is not always appreciated just what a political tightrope he had to walk. His predecessor, Herwald Ramsbotham, had been removed largely because of what the Prime Minister held to be over-enthusiastic advocacy of reforms pressed upon him by senior civil servants. Butler succeeded him knowing that he would have to be seen to be running his department. An Anglican from a family which had many connections with higher education, he established an excellent relationship with Chuter Ede, a Unitarian who had taught in elementary schools before the First World War and who is probably one of the most under-rated personalities in English educational history. Butler relied upon Chuter Ede's knowledge of the world of local government to facilitate the abolition of the 1902 Act's 'Part III authorities' and such was the importance which he attached to Ede's support that he actually persuaded him in February 1942, as Ede's diary records, to turn down an offer of promotion to another department. The Permanent Secretary, (Sir) Maurice Holmes, on whose judgement too Butler came to rely heavily, was also from a family which had connections with education. His father was a distinguished chief inspector of elementary schools who had written *What Is and What Might Be*, published in 1911. With his deputy, R.S. Wood, Holmes had come to realize that the Board of Education tended to respond to stimuli rather than to create discussion. Burdened as they were with everyday administration, the Board's senior staff had failed to engage in effective policy-making. As Wood put it in a note to his superior in November 1940, the power of Board officers had been seriously eroded in the past twenty years (Gosden, 1981, pp. 92–3). This was the thinking behind the discussion document produced by the Board's senior officials just before Butler's appointment. Entitled *Education after the War*,

21

but known as the Green Book from the colour of its cover, it was supposed to be confidential; as W.O. Lester Smith, chief education officer for Manchester, wryly remarked, it had been 'distributed in such a blaze of secrecy that it achieved an unusual degree of publicity' (Smith, 1942, p. 155). Butler quickly made the contents of the Green Book widely known. Despite discouragement from the Prime Minister, who was anxious both to avoid any repetition of the bitter controversies which had occurred over the 1902 Act and to prevent the kind of political heat which had been aroused in 1918 over the question of the public schools, Butler resolved to formulate an Education Bill which would ensure the adaptation of the English educational system to modern requirements and make a contribution to the restoration of social stability after the War. It was Butler himself who overcame the objections of his cabinet and party colleagues to educational reform and persuaded them to give priority to education as against other social measures, notably the Beveridge scheme of social welfare. He had the advantage over Beveridge that he was advocating a relatively cheap reform; as Butler noted in his diary in September 1943, 'there is a feeling that Beveridge ... wishes to give away a great deal of other people's money' (Jeffereys, 1984, p. 426). Thus did he achieve what Dent called 'the greatest measure of educational advance since 1870, and probably the greatest ever known' (Simon, 1986, p. 31).

It was in part the exigencies of war which stimulated this reform. In early 1940 half a million children in this country were deprived of education for a period because of the upheaval created by the evacuation of children from the cities and the recruitment of teachers for active service. The evacuation exercise revealed just how variable educational provision was between one area and another and just how great was the social divide between the different classes and the different districts in England and Wales. This message had been enunciated by many people in the 1930s, and indeed before, by none more effectively than by the Socialist economic historian R.H. Tawney, who commented in 1929:

Even in childhood, different strata of the population are distinguished by sharp contrasts of environment, of health and of physical well-being ... The great majority are exposed to conditions in which health, if not impossible, is necessarily precarious, and end their education just at the age when their powers are beginning to develop.

(Tawney, 1964, p. 74)

Already in 1940 and 1941 the Board of Education was being much criticized for failing to plan adequately for the needs of the schools in wartime and for failing to assert leadership which would have precluded the wide disparity of provision between local authorities. Pressure was clearly on for a larger measure of centralization in English education and for a move towards equality of educational opportunity for every child, with all that implied by way of extra resources. The evident concern for reform shown by the officials of the Board of Education was perhaps partly due to a conviction that more radical demands would be made at the conclusion of the War if substantial advances were not made during it.

The raising of the school-leaving age to 15, which had been planned for 1 September 1939, and the creation of free secondary education for all, as proposed in the Spens Report of 1938, were clearly essential steps. In a speech to the Conference of the National Union of Teachers on 9 April 1942, Butler put forward proposals which the Union's President declared 'the most progressive ever outlined by a President of the Board of Education'. This was surely the apogee of harmony between central government and the teaching profession in Britain. Butler openly sought to create a partnership between government and teachers, which the teachers' leaders, led by the charismatic Ronald Gould of the National Union of Teachers, found flattering. One consequence was that they put their members' responsibilities above their rights and thus raised the standing of the profession in the eyes of the general public. What Butler proposed was in effect a radical reorganization; he called for an education system providing a 'training suited to talents' for every child, for the introduction of training for industry coupled with a

23

modified system of apprenticeship, and for the provision of continued education on a part-time basis. It was a bold plan.

What Butler did not enlarge upon in April 1942, and what was to prove the most time-consuming aspect of his reform, was the future of the 'dual system' of provided and non-provided schools. As recently as 1902, it must be remembered, the National Society (for Promoting the Education of the Poor in the Principles of the Established Church) had nearly 12,000 schools in England and Wales and the voluntary or Church schools of all kinds were educating two and a half million children as against the two and a quarter million in Board or maintained schools. By the 1940s, however, many of the voluntary schools were in a sorry physical state — few new voluntary schools had been built in the twentieth century and the Church of England, for example, had not found it possible to respond effectively to the building requirements represented by the Hadow reorganization. In 1944, 92 per cent of Church school buildings dated from before 1902. Moreover, especially in the rural areas, a large number of voluntary schools were too small to be efficient; many were one-teacher schools.

There remained deep divisions among churchmen of all creeds as to the best solution to the problem. Clearly, no settlement was feasible without the full co-operation of the Church of England, the free churches, the Roman Catholic community, the local administrators and the teachers. In 1941 and 1942 the interests of these various parties seemed too diverse and conflicting to be reconciled. One factor promoted a large degree of unity among Anglicans and Free Churchmen, if not among Roman Catholics — the 'agreed syllabus' of religious instruction pioneered in Cambridgeshire from 1924. Butler put forward the solution of a choice of status for Church schools, to become either 'controlled' or 'aided'. Controlled schools would have the nature of their religious instruction safeguarded but the local education authority would be responsible for all the costs and for the appointment of the teachers other than those for religious instruction. Aided schools would have their teachers' salaries and their running expenses met by the local authority and an Exchequer grant towards building costs, but the managers would be in charge of the buildings, appointments to the teaching staff and the religious instruction. This proposed solution was incorporated in the White Paper of 1 July 1943, which preceded the Education Bill by a matter of six months and so allowed for ample public discussion. *The Times Educational Supplement* hailed the proposal as an 'ingenious and intricate compromise' and, although the Roman Catholics never accepted the financial basis for voluntary school building which at the time provided for half of the cost from central government funds, even they became reconciled to the religious basis of the settlement. The Act provided for a corporate act of worship at the start of each school day in maintained schools and for the freedom of parents to withdraw their children from religious instruction. What probably contributed as much as anything to the achievement of a settlement in this sensitive area was the personal regard which Butler had for William Temple, Archbishop of Canterbury 1942–4, and for Cardinal Griffin, Archbishop of Westminster from 1943, a respect which was, one suspects, fully reciprocated. Temple was probably as important in 1944 as the Cowper–Temple clause had been in 1870.

It is wrong, however, to imagine that the 1944 Education Act constituted nothing but concession to vested interests. Fears were expressed during the passage of the Bill, inside and outside Parliament, that the proposed powers for the Minister for Education were too extensive. There was a clear intention to establish a strong Ministry to control the local education authorities in a manner which would have been unthinkable twenty years before in the time of Lord Eustace Percy. Section 1 of the Act unequivocally put an awesome responsibility on the Secretary of State:

> to promote the education of the people of England and Wales and the progressive development of institutions devoted to that purpose and to secure the effective execution by local authorities, under his control and direction, of the national policy for providing a varied and comprehensive educational service in every area.

When Butler stated that he intended central government to 'lead

25

boldly and not to follow timidly' he was warmly applauded in the Commons, but he was at pains to emphasize that there was no intention of diminishing or destroying the former spirit of partnership between central government and local authorities. It was, of course, a crucial consideration and Edward Short, Secretary of State for Education from 1968 to 1970, was to speak almost a generation later of

> the dilemma in education all the time, the desire to preserve some kind of order and authority, but at the same time to preserve academic freedom and a certain amount of autonomy. I think this applies within institutions, it applies in the distribution of power in the system as well. This is the basic problem in organizing education nationally in a free society.
>
> (Evidence to Select Committee on Education and Science 1968–9, vol. II, question 1378)

The reduction under the 1944 Act of the existing 315 local education authorities to 146 meant that the authorities were generally larger and more powerful than they had been. Nevertheless, there is no gainsaying that the 1944 Act was intended to ensure uniform, or at any rate nearly uniform, national standards in education and to control maverick local education authorities. Section 68 specifically gave the Minister the power to discipline local authorities who stepped out of line:

> If the Secretary of State is satisfied either on complaint by any person or otherwise that any local education authority or the managers or governors of any county or voluntary school have acted or are proposing to act unreasonably with respect to the exercise of any power conferred or the performance of any duty imposed or under this Act, he may, notwithstanding any enactment rendering the exercise of the power or the performance of the duty contingent upon the opinion of the authority and of the managers or governors, give such directions as to the exercise of the power or performance of the duty as appear to him to be expedient.

Butler's approach embodied the idea that the proper relationship between central government and what happened in the locality was represented by the definition of an education service as 'a national service locally administered'. It was, of course, right to recognize that national policy had to be adapted to accommodate the variety of geographical and demographic factors at work in the country, but the Minister was intended to give firm leadership. Unfortunately, in the first twenty and more years after the Act successive ministers and senior civil servants failed to exert that leadership. Consequently, when the idea of a partnership broke down, as it did in 1976 when the Secretary of State held Tameside authority to be unreasonable for not proceeding with comprehensive reorganization, the judges held the Minister's discretion, as allowed by the 1944 Act, to be inconsistent with the Common Law. As a result they imposed such severe tests for the justification of ministerial intervention that the force of the Act was undermined.

Butler's plans to provide the Minister with more help in formulating educational policies were more successful. The Act established Central Advisory Councils, for England and Wales respectively, composed of distinguished educationists and representatives of other interested parties. These councils were the successors to the Consultative Committee on Education which had existed since the beginning of the century but their role was different in an important respect. The Consultative Committee had only been able to proffer advice when it was sought; the Advisory Councils could take the initiative and offer advice as necessary. This they did very effectively, producing the Crowther Report, *15 to 18*, in 1959 and the Newsom Report, *Half Our Future*, in 1963, both of which had far-reaching influence in the education service. Just how broadly the Central Advisory Council for England interpreted its role may be judged from the statement of the first chairman, Sir Fred Clarke, that he looked forward to a 'much more thoroughly collectivist' order of society in which schools were to be unified. The Newsom Report made a clear statement on the Council's philosophical position:

> The future pattern of employment in this country will require a much larger pool of talent than is at present available; and that at least a substantial proportion of the 'average' and 'below average' pupils are sufficiently educable to supply that additional talent. The need is not

27

only for more skilled workers to fill existing jobs, but also for a generally educated and intelligently adaptable labour force to meet new demands. (*Half Our Future*, ch. I, paras. 3–8)

Despite the initiatives of the Advisory Councils, the Minister was the dominant partner in education through his control of most educational resources and his possession of an administrative apparatus in the Ministry and in the Inspectorate which allowed his influence to be felt the length and breadth of the land. Constitutionally, he was responsible to Parliament and people for every action of his Department, but the Ministry of Education was held to be not so much an executive agency as a policy-making body, operating by influence — particularly through the distribution of resources. Apart from the controls exercised by means of regulations, orders and circulars, the Ministry of Education relied very much in the years immediately after 1944 on the influence which it could exert on the local education authorities and on the teaching profession. It must not be forgotten, either, that the Ministry's officials exerted a definite influence on the successive Secretaries of State which it is difficult to delineate but which was clearly — and rightly — considerable. As the former Head of the Civil Service put it in 1950: 'It is ... precisely on these broad issues (of policy) that it is the duty of a civil servant to give his minister the fullest benefit of the storehouse of departmental expertise' (Bridges, 1950, p. 19). At the end of the day, however, as Sir William Pile, Permanent Secretary at the Department of Education and Science, 1970 to 1976, has pointed out:

Ministers, and occasionally officials, by personal characteristics like clarity of mind, strength of character or instinctive tactical skills, have made distinctive contributions to the shaping of events. But in the matter of objectives, and often of the means to those ends, they have themselves been shaped by more deep seated forces. The obscure tides of moral, social and economic change which have run with singular strength in the post-war years have in this sense been the main determining factors. (Pile, 1979, ch. 15)

Besides making the Minister more powerful than ever before, the Act had incorporated the principle of parental involvement in a novel, if not very effective, way. Section 76, essentially the result of a House of Lords amendment, stated:

> The Secretary of State and local education authorities shall have regard to the general principle that, so far as is compatible with the provision of efficient instruction and training and the avoidance of unreasonable public expenditure, pupils are to be educated in accordance with the wishes of their parents.

During the years of the Depression many working-class parents who wanted their children to have a more advanced education than they had enjoyed themselves had been obliged to refuse places at grammar schools on financial grounds because even the extras of school uniforms and sports equipment had been beyond their pockets. But in the brave new world after 1944 parents were to have a voice in the growth of educational provision. Alienation from education by large proportions of ordinary people, exemplified by the Marbenton youth's comment on his local grammar school, 'What a bloody way to grow up!', was increasingly replaced by an aspiration that all should have the opportunity of a grammar school education. Even so, the Organization for Economic Co-operation and Development report *Educational Development Strategy in England and Wales* (1975) held the Ministry to be 'undoubtedly the most important single force in determining the direction and tempo of educational development'.

Only five sections of the 1944 Act related to central administration as against forty-two which were concerned with local administration, and it was the local education authorities who took the initiative in implementing the Act as far as school education was concerned, particularly through their association, the Association of Education Committees. All local education committees, with the single exception of the London County Council and later the Inner London Education Authority, belonged to the Association. William Alexander, the former Education Officer for Margate and Sheffield, was its Secretary, a dynamic personality who had an almost mesmeric effect upon councillors and officers. Local authorities were required under the Act to establish education committees 'for the efficient discharge of their functions with respect to education'; and these committees, because they spent a major portion of the author-ities' budgets, were very powerful. The Association proved a most effective political force at a time when education was taking a markedly increased share of the nation's resources. In 1938 it had 3 per cent of the Gross National Product; in 1961 4.5 per cent; and in 1975 7 per cent. Between 1945 and the election of the Labour government in 1964, there existed not only a general consensus in the country at large that education was 'a good thing', that the system had to be reconstructed and that the increasing number of children from a rising birthrate and from raising the school-leaving age had to be accommodated, but an acceptance that 'some things are better fixed up by officers behind closed doors, without a cry of "foul" going up' (Maclure, 1985, p. 124). One of the causes of the education committees' strength was that the Act established a separate central government percentage grant for education. This arrangement was brought to an end in 1958 with the imposition of a block grant system. In theory, a block grant allows the level of central contribution to be varied more readily than a percentage grant; any new expenditure under a block grant falls on the rates. By 1958 the total of government grants to local government had become more than the total of local rates, and rates had only doubled since the beginning of the Second World War, whereas incomes had nearly trebled. The Treasury clearly hoped to reduce central contribu-tions and increase local input, but in practice the Minister lost the flexibility of control possible under a percentage grant and the reliance implied by a block grant on financial yardsticks based on average costs led to an increased, instead of a decreased, variation in the standards of educational provision. As a leader in *Education* on 15 February 1957 put it:

It will be necessary throughout to ask if the revision of the grant procedures as far as education is concerned, at least, is going to be in the best interests of the children in the school. Or is this designed to restore the financial climate of the inter-war years to the world of education?

It had been a basic tenet of the thinking behind the 1944 Act that educational opportunity should as far as possible be independent of social class or place of birth. It was a principle which was abandoned, not for the first or last time in English educational history, in the face of economic expediency. The long-term consequence was that education was demoted in status to be a local service comparable with any other, instead of a national service of vital importance. This was to be significant when local government itself came to be reformed in 1972–4. It was a major achievement of the education service in the twenty years after the 1944 Act to provide sufficient school buildings to ensure every child a secondary education in a school either specifically built or brought up to standard for that purpose as well as catering for the education at all levels of an increasing number of children. In 1947 there were 5,034,725 pupils in maintained schools in England and Wales; in 1965 7,092,155. The successful provision was the result of effective co-operation between central government and the local authorities.

A committee had been established to consider the problems of post-war school building even while the 1944 Act was being prepared and by 1951 12 per cent of the circulars (over 240) issued by the new Ministry of Education had been concerned with school building, notably Circular 10: *Draft Building Regulations* and Circular 28: *Preparation of Development Plans*. Development plans exercised the minds of local authorities and it is clear that the provision of 'Secondary Education for All' was very much more than a matter of changing the names of schools, even where an authority had recent purpose-built senior elementary schools. To provide buildings which met the new regulations, authorities had to acquire great areas of land and, that done, schemes were soon frustrated by shortages of labour and material resulting from the competition between housing and education and by general economic cuts in the face of rollicking public expenditure. Ellen Wilkinson, in one of her last acts as Minister for Education before her premature death in February 1947, persuaded the Cabinet to agree that the educational and political advantages of introducing the raising of the school-leaving age on 1 April 1947 outweighed any possible economic gains from deferment but her successors, faced with continual difficulties over providing premises, were not always so sanguine. By June 1952 the Association of Education Committees was expressing deep concern 'lest the restrictions on school buildings force lower standards in educational provision'. By June 1953 William Alexander was writing in *Education*:

> There has of late been considerable criticism of the work of the school. When the conditions in which school work has to be undertaken are fully appreciated it is a matter of great congratulation that so much successful work has been undertaken despite the adverse conditions which obtain.

A survey conducted by the Association in 1952 had established that in the counties 86,496 rural and 62,555 urban places and in county boroughs 76,901 places were required simply to do away with all-age schools. Seven years later, a writer in *Education* was still complaining of 'the repeated failure of the local authorities to start the full allocated programme within the years of allocation'. In January 1963 there were still 55,226 pupils aged 11 and over in all-age schools, a problem not to be resolved until 1972.

The story of building provision from 1944 to 1964 is not all depressing. The Ministry's development group for school building stimulated innovative means of construction. Authorities learnt that even in areas affected by subsidence, like parts of Nottinghamshire, schools could be quickly and safely erected from standardized prefabricated materials. In 1957 the Ministry brought about the co-ordination of six local authorities with subsidence problems — the Consortium of Local Authorities Special Programme (CLASP). Shropshire local education authority pioneered SCOLA, another consortium for building schools as rapidly and efficiently as possible. W.K. Richmond has argued that in the period after 1949 the Ministry's Building Bulletins 'must be reckoned one of the most potent influences in transforming the primary school's way of life'. The sheer flair of architectural imagination which produced such exciting plans stimulated fresh concepts of teaching. *Building Bulletin 36*, for example, contained seven pages of photographs and captions setting out the theoretical principles behind the architects' plans, e.g.: 'In primary schools every surface is a work surface, including the floor on which individuals may erect and contrive complex structures.' As Richmond comments, 'Given working conditions as spacious and gracious as these, it would be hard for a teacher not to adopt a developmental approach even if she or he had never so much as heard of Piaget and was totally unfamiliar with the practice of team-teaching' (1978, p. 44).

Teachers and teacher trainers, that much maligned group, brought about a revolution in the approach to children's learning in the environments which the Ministry's architects created, especially in the new primary schools. That revolution was well summed up by Sybil Marshall in 1963 when she called for an end to 'two by four' education — the kind of learning confined to what was between the two covers of a book and the four walls of a classroom (Marshall, 1963, *passim*: see especially the illustrations).

George Tomlinson, Secretary of State for Education in 1947, is reputed to have said, 'the Minister knows nowt about curriculum'. In no other western democracy has there existed the measure of curricular freedom which has been traditional in England. Back in 1906 the Board of Education in its significantly titled *Handbook of Suggestions for Teachers* had declared:

> The only uniformity that the Board of Education desires to see in the teaching of public elementary schools is that each teacher should think for himself and work out for himself such methods of teaching as may use his powers to best advantage and be best suited to the particular needs and conditions of the school.
> (Board of Education, 1906, *Prefatory Memorandum*)

In the twenty years after the 1944 Act local education authorities were content to follow the model articles of government for their schools put forward in the schedule to *Administrative Memorandum no. 25* of 1945:

> The Local Education Authority shall determine the general

33

educational character of the school and its place in the local educational system. Subject thereto, the governors shall have the general direction of the conduct and curriculum of the school.

In practice, the head and the staff determined curriculum content; the governors concurred; the local authority exercised only indirect means of control — by the provision of funds and buildings, by its determination of the establishment of the teaching and auxiliary staff, by its influence on appointments and promotions, and by the advice of its inspectors. Central government exercised only a rather nebulous influence through Her Majesty's Inspectors, who disseminated instances of good practice and published national reports the role of which was somewhat rhetorical. Not that Government's rhetorical role is to be discounted. Easen (1975, p. 161) estimated that in 1930 it took fifteen years for something like 3 per cent of schools to adopt a recommended change, by 1960 seven years for 11 per cent of schools to do so. It must be remembered, too, that the advisory staff of local education authorities as well as subject associations and other teachers' organizations play a part in accomplishing the curriculum change adumbrated by HMIs or by a national report.

Local authorities were equally allowed much freedom in determining the particular form of organization of schools best suited to their circumstances. The 1944 Act did not impose any rigid structure at primary or secondary level. What some have regarded as the Act's key clause reads:

> The statutory system of public education shall be organized in three progressive stages to be known as primary education, secondary education, and further education; and it shall be the duty of the local education authority for every area, so far as their powers extend, to contribute towards the spiritual, mental and physical development of the community by securing that efficient education throughout those stages shall be available to meet the needs of the population of their area. (Part II, 7)

There was no statutory requirement for nursery education. The Board of Education Report for 1938 had been obliged to admit that little progress had been made in nursery provision between the wars; 13 schools in 1918 had risen to 30 by 1938. The 1944 Act permitted the establishment of nursery classes but the percentage of children under five did not materially increase between the 1930s and the 1960s. Primary education was considered to begin at 5, secondary deliberately vaguely set as between ten and a half and 12, and schools would 'not be deemed to be sufficient unless they … afford for all pupils opportunities for education offering such variety … as may be desirable in view of their different ages, abilities and aptitudes'. Butler's chief parliamentary draughtsman, Sir Grenville Ram, had told him that the Act would meet the needs of at least a generation 'provided it did not seek to exclude experiments with multilateral schools' (James, 1980, p. 72). The Act neither laid down a tripartite system of secondary education nor precluded the organization of secondary education on comprehensive lines. Indeed, in the 1940s and 1950s ministers, even Labour ministers, were reluctant to pronounce in favour of secondary school reorganization. Ellen Wilkinson, the Minister for Education in the 1945 Labour Government, 'was to show scant sympathy with pressure … in favour of a multi-lateral or comprehensive system of secondary education. Nor did she accept the view common on the left that the tripartite division … was socially and education-ally divisive' (Morgan, 1984, p. 175).

After all, when Professor Godfrey Thomson had advised the Northumberland County Council to introduce an 11-plus examination in the 1920s, he had been working for democratic reform: the identification of working-class children who could benefit from selective secondary education. Furthermore, many local authorities were loath to introduce educational reorgani-zation which would necessitate large-scale building costs, and they could justify their reluctance by pointing to Butler's insistence that no stigma should attach to secondary schools which were not grammar schools. The aim was to have equivalent, if different, physical provision in each of the types of secondary school: grammar, modern and technical. The White Paper of 1943 had further stated that these different schools were not necessarily to remain 'separate and apart. Different types may be combined in one building or on one site.' It may have been, as Sir Fred Clarke wrote of the Spens proposals, 'a little naive to imagine that in the present state of English society real parity of status can be established between the "modern" school for the unselected goats and the "grammar" school for the carefully selected sheep' (Clarke, 1940, pp. 45–46), but the high degree of autonomy accorded to heads and their staffs meant that individual schools really could determine their internal organization and deploy their resources (such as promotion points) at their own discretion if they had, as most had, a compliant governing body. They could also introduce innovations as, for example, many secondary moderns did in respect of taking public examinations or producing pupil profiles to help prospective employers at selection interviews. In a period of expansion and of euphoria over the efficacy of education, individual schools no less than local authorities enjoyed very real freedom of manoeuvre.

London County Council decided as early as July 1944 on a scheme of partial comprehensive organization and published a London School Plan in 1947. The Education Officer, Sir Graham Savage, had been impressed by American common high schools and the cost of land in London encouraged economy of scale. But the first purpose-built comprehensive school was not opened in London until 1954. Planned to accommodate 2,000 girls, Kidbrooke School's opening was intended to be accompanied by the closure of several older secondary schools in the catchment area including Eltham Hill, a girls' grammar school, but a parents' petition to Miss Florence Horsburgh, Minister for Education, led to a ruling against such closure. By 1954 Anglesey had a complete system of comprehensive secondary schools and by 1960 there were 130 comprehensive schools in England and Wales where in 1950 there had been 10. A large measure of freedom to experiment was left to the teaching staff. As Raymond King, an influential head at Wandsworth, wrote on his retirement in 1964, it was 'the highest tribute ever paid by an education authority to its teachers to leave them virtually free to build up the great comprehensives in the way they judged best'. (Simon, 1985, p. 164).

While most local education authorities had separatist plans, several created 'school bases' with different types of secondary school on the same site, as did Bolton and Brighton, and others established bi-lateral schools (grammar–technical or technical–modern), as did Barrow-in-Furness and Berkshire. Many Labour-controlled authorities proved determined to retain grammar schools (Durham in the event was among the last to introduce comprehensive plans) while West Wales, controlled by the Liberals, and Westmorland, controlled by the Conservatives, were among the first to go comprehensive. Secondary modern schools often enough made an impressive contribution to the progress of their pupils and the number staying on voluntarily beyond the school-leaving age rose from 9,000 in 1949 to 21,000 in 1957, while the number of secondary modern pupils sitting the General Certificate of Education at O Level rose from 5,500 in 1954 to 55,000 in 1964. H.C. Dent has declared, 'The twenty years following 1945 saw in the Secondary Modern school a process of evolution unmatched for speed and significance in the history of English education' (Dent, 1969b, p. 118).

Secondary technical schools, on the other hand, never stood a chance of full acceptance. Although *The New Secondary Education* (Ministry of Education, 1947) held them to cater for a minority of able children who are likely to make their best response when the curriculum is strongly coloured by industrial and commercial interests, the secondary technical school suffered from the indifference of most local authorities (Rotherham was an honourable exception), from recruiting at the age of twelve or thirteen, by which time the brighter pupils of that age were settled in grammar schools, and from sharing premises in most instances with a technical college. Less than 4 per cent of the age group attended secondary technical schools by 1958. By the late 1950s the consensus which had been so beneficial to the education service from the time of the 1944 Act was beginning to wear thin. Support for the comprehensive principle gradually grew within the Labour Party, but up to 1964 it was still predominantly a demand for gradualism in organizational change. Confidence in the system was undermined by sociologists rather than by politicians or educationists. The Central Advisory Council report on *Early Leaving* in 1954 found that where there should have been 927 children in its grammar-school sample, to match the proportion in the population at large, there were only 436, two-thirds of whom left without three passes at O Level (Ministry of Education, 1954, pp. 34–5). The Crowther Report in 1959 identified three major factors affecting the education of young people aged 15 to 19: the 'bulge' of rising birthrate, the 'trend' to stay on at school and the 'swing' from arts to science. More importantly it looked for systematic sociological explanations of the distribution of educational opportunity and analysed some of the major social influences on educability. The work of Jean Floud, A.H. Halsey and F.M. Martin, who published the influential study *Social Class and Educational Opportunity* in 1956, demonstrated that the widening of educational provision did not necessarily reduce social inequalities in educational opportunity and that the proportion of children from economically deprived homes receiving a grammar school education was not markedly greater than it had been a whole generation before. The proportion of grammar school places available varied from 10 to over 40 per cent in England and reached 60 per cent in parts of Wales, but the national average was just over 20 per cent in 1956 and nine out of ten children in the lowest social stratum did not gain a grammar school place. Moreover, the White Paper *Secondary Education for All* (1958) stated that between 10 and 20 per cent of primary children aged eleven were wrongly allocated to grammar and secondary modern schools. The sociologists' findings were a blow to those who had believed that school reform could bring about social reform and economic growth. As Professor Gosden has pointed out:

Possibly the greatest contrast between the pre-war and post-war situation was the much greater willingness of central and local authorities to spend far more on education in real terms ... The predominant attitude came to be one of expecting a measure of growth in expenditure from one year to another.

(Gosden, 1976, p. 433)

Retrenchment was not, however, to come yet. This was particularly true of further and higher education of all kinds. The local authorities were slow to respond to their statutory duty under the 1944 Act to provide for further education and by 1955 there were only five times as many day-release students as in 1938 and the number of full-time students had little more than trebled. This was despite a decided awareness of the importance of vocationally oriented education for the future of the economy in the years immediately after the War. The Percy Report of 1945 on higher technological education called for the production of 1,500 engineers annually from selected technical colleges up to 1955 and the Barlow Report of 1946, in forecasting scientific manpower needs, recommended the immediate doubling of the output of scientific manpower. By 1955 the technical colleges were in fact producing 4,000 engineers and some colleges were using extraordinary stratagems to do so. Grants for capital improvements and maintenance had been increased to 75 per cent for colleges offering courses in advanced technology but international technological competition made it clear that much more was needed. The White Paper *Technical Education* (Ministry of Education, 1956) outlined an 'alternative and much broader road' than the universities offered and called for the concentration of advanced courses in 'colleges of advanced technology'. Ten CATS were eventually designated and from 1962 received grants directly from the Ministry of Education, but industry was not always ready to accept the Diploma in Technology, which they awarded from 1955 under the supervision of the National Council for Technological Awards, as a degree-equivalent. Between 1956 and 1961 central government provided increased grants, local authorities made maintenance grants at university rates, and industry made more use of sandwich courses. It was co-operative control of a major educational expansion: between 1954 and 1962 the number of full-time students in further education, that is technical and art colleges and colleges of commerce, increased from 36,000 to 114,000, and the number of part-time students from 251,000 to 454,000. Even so, public attitudes determined that the other pupils in schools looked to pure rather than applied science courses and it was the less able who were steered into technology and engineering.

The Barlow Committee had commented in 1946: 'It is only to the universities that we can look for any substantial recruitment to the ranks of qualified scientists ... Generally speaking, the university is an essential stage in scientists' education' (Barlow Report, 1946, p. 6). The university sector expanded very considerably from 1946. The University Grants Committee (UGC) effectively controlled the size and nature of that expansion, for instance, insisting on a 'foundation year' for all students before approving the creation of the University College of North Staffordshire in 1950, although it was the Treasury which made the finance available. Where £6.9 million was spent on 77,000 university students in 1946–7, £28 million was provided for 94,000 students in 1955–6 and this was to rise to £122 million in 1965–6. Numerous university charters were granted in the period — to former university colleges at Nottingham (1948), Southampton (1952), Hull (1954), Exeter (1955) and Leicester (1957) while Sussex (1961) was the prototype of a new kind of university (the 'plateglass' model) where the compartmentalization of subject disciplines was abandoned in favour of more integrated courses. In 1920 government and local authority grants had provided only two-sevenths of universities' income; in 1955 they were responsible for over two-thirds.

The UGC had been charged in 1946 with preparing and executing 'such plans for the development of the universities as may from time to time be required in order to ensure that they are fully adequate to national needs'. The instrument of control was the quinquennial grant system. Indeed, in 1963 John Vaizey declared the quinquennial grant system 'a *sine qua non* of the methods of influence developed by the UGC that the existing non-interference in matters of detail should be maintained' (Vaizey, 1963, p. 169). In 1956 the Committee set a target of 168,000 university students by 1968.

Teacher training also expanded. Section 62 of the 1944 Act had laid the responsibility very firmly on the Minister to:

> make such arrangements as he considers expedient for securing that there shall be available sufficient facilities for the training of teachers ... and ... give to any local education authority such directions as he thinks necessary requiring them to establish, maintain, or assist any training college.

The McNair Report (1944) had called for a closer association for colleges with universities 'to resist the encroachments of centralization' and, after much division of opinion and debate, area training organizations had been created in 1948 based on institutes of education associated with most universities. Miss E.C. Oakden, HMI, the much respected assistant secretary to the McNair Committee, later recalled that 'many educational discussions, by no means confined to McNair, turned on the dangers of the substance of educational learning falling under the control of central and political government' (Niblett et al., 1975, p. 112). Immediately after the War, there was a pressing demand for teachers to staff the schools in preparation for the raising of the school-leaving age and the Emergency Training Scheme in 1947, at its peak, was producing 13,500 students a year from 55 specially created colleges housed in anything from hutted hostels to mediaeval castles. Meanwhile the normal two-year training was being expanded with the aid of increased government grants and by 1951 56 voluntary and 76 local authority colleges had 25,000 students in training. By 1960 the increased number of teacher trainees allowed the course to be extended to three years and, as *Pamphlet 34* had stressed in 1957, it was accepted as 'important for the health of the teaching profession as a whole that three-year teacher training should give a considerable proportion of teachers an academic standing and confidence which will enable them to take their place alongside graduates' (*Pamphlet 34*, 1957).

In November 1960 the Government, recognizing that the huge changes in tertiary education merited a full-scale enquiry, appointed a committee under Lord Robbins to advise on both short-term and long-term solutions to the problem of providing skilled manpower. In its report in 1963, the Committee acknowledged:

> Higher education has not been planned as a whole or developed within a framework consciously devised to promote harmonious evolution. What system there is has come about as the result of a series of particular initiatives, concerned with particular needs and particular situations. (*Robbins Report*, 1963, para. 18)

The Committee held that '[the view that] there exists some easy method of ascertaining an intelligence factor unaffected by education or background is outmoded'. Its chairman told the Lords that where 45 per cent of children from higher professional families were entering higher education, only 4 per cent from skilled manual families were doing so. Much of the evidence submitted to the Committee was concerned with the right kind of institutional structure for the expanded higher education clientele. Public expectation was raised to a quite new level of aspiration and even the projected increases in student numbers in higher education in Great Britain from 216,000 in 1962 to over 390,000 in 1973 and nearly 560,000 in 1980 were soon held to be underestimates. Few would have disagreed at the time with the Committee's contention in paragraph 630 of its report: 'As an investment, there seems a strong presumption in favour of a substantially increased expenditure on higher education'.

In 1944 the aim had been secondary education for all. Such was the impact of the thinking behind the 1944 Act and of the changes which had been accomplished in its wake that by 1964 the aim was seriously mooted of higher education of some kind for all. This high ideal was not destined to be achieved but credit must be given that it existed even as a notion. The Butler Act had marked a real watershed in the history of English education; from then dates the concept that every child is entitled as a right, and not as a privilege, to such education as he or she can demonstrate having the capacity to use.

But from an early stage Butler had decided that one area of privilege must not be involved in any legislation or in any radical reform — the public schools. By referring the question of their future to the Fleming Committee in July 1942, which he instructed 'to consider means whereby the association between the public schools ... and the general educational system of the country could be developed and extended', he hoped that the matter would be placed outside controversy until after his Bill had become law. He had more success in this than he could possibly have anticipated. For in the early years of the War, when many held that the Battle of Britain had been won on the playing fields of the county grammar schools as much as the Battle of Waterloo had been won on the playing fields of Eton, there was much discussion among teacher and local authority organizations and especially in the Association of Directors and Secretaries of Education and in Labour Party groups of the integration of the public schools into the maintained system. As the Workers' Education Association put it in its *Plan for Education* (1942): 'Democracy must itself take possession of the public schools.' Sir Fred Clarke had expressed a widely held view when he wrote in 1940: 'We can hardly continue to contemplate an England where the mass of the people coming on by one education path are to be governed for the most part by a minority advancing along a quite separate and more favoured path.' It was no coincidence that the Fleming Report was published two months after the Butler Bill was given its third reading and one week before the Royal Assent. 'The first class carriage had been shunted on to an immense siding,' as Butler himself commented in his memoirs (Butler, 1982, p. 120). The Report in fact aroused little interest. Its most interesting proposal was that independent schools should reserve at least 25 per cent of their places for pupils from maintained primary schools who would be selected by local education authorities. Few local authorities made any arrangements at all to place children in public schools and, whereas in 1939 the financial position of many had been decidedly weak, after the War the schools enjoyed a new prosperity. They could afford to ignore the attacks upon their position which came from such critics as T.C. Worsley: 'We are where we are, and shall be where we shall be, owing, largely if not wholly, to the privileged education which the ruling classes have received in the last forty years' (Worsley, 1940, p. 274). Harold Silver has put their situation well: 'The fee-paying schools have continued ever since to exist on a borderline of discussion between the injustice of privilege and freedom in a democracy' (Silver, 1980, p. 23).

3 Educational development in an age of politicization, 1964–79

Faith in education's value

The metamorphosis of the Ministry of Education into the Department of Education and Science in 1964 'marked a high point in public faith in the virtues of education' (Barnes, 1977, p. 15). The belief in the significance of educational advance for the future welfare of Britain was to last until the publication of the White Paper *Framework for Expansion* in 1972 which stated categorically:

> The last ten years have seen a major expansion of the education service. The next ten will see expansion continue — as it must if education is to make its full contribution to the vitality of our society and our economy.

The expansion of educational provision in the thirty years after the Second World War was very real. In 1938 education had taken only 3 per cent of the Gross National Product; in 1975 it took 7 per cent. In 1938–9 defence accounted for 20 and education for 8 per cent of public expenditure; in 1974–5 the proportions were respectively 9 and 12 per cent. In the 1930s one in a hundred of young people in England and Wales went on to full-time higher education; in 1975 one in seven. In 1938–9 there were just under 40,000 further education students; in 1974–5 approximately 400,000. At the end of the War there were, in round figures, five million pupils in maintained schools; in 1975 nine million, and in that time the number of teachers in schools, colleges and universities trebled.

Controversy over comprehension

If, however, there was agreement on the value of education, the consensus approach to the nature of provision which was appropriate was to break down in the later 1960s, particularly over secondary schooling. By 1970, Sir Toby Weaver commented:

> It is a sad feature of the current educational scene that in the eyes of those who champion them, these methods [of teaching] have become polarised towards the two ends of the spectrum. The advocates of 'child-centredness' pronounce themselves 'progressives' and excoriate those who emphasise the other end of the spectrum as shell-backed 'traditionalists'. The discipline-centred retaliate with the charge that their opponents are soft-centred activity-methodists. The embattled paper tigers, empanoplied in red and black, raise their banners, shout slogans and go to silly war. (Weaver, 1970, p. 25)

Weaver wrote this lament after the publication of the first of three collections of Black Papers (Cox and Boyson, 1971), essays by academics and others which called for a return to traditional teaching and which constituted a response to the philosophy epitomized in the Plowden Report, *Children and Their Primary Schools* (1967). This Report, the last major contribution of the Central Advisory Council for Education (England), gave positive endorsement to pupil-chosen activity rather than to class teaching, commended project work, centres of interest, and integration of subject matter, deprecated extrinsic as against intrinsic rewards, encouraged group work and discouraged punishment, and sponsored the policy options of middle schools for pupils aged 8 to 12 and of positive discrimination in the designation of Educational Priority Areas.

Pedagogy was one area of controversy; the organization of schools, especially secondary schools, was another and of even wider public concern. By the mid-1960s local authorities were beginning to make primary education a priority. The Ministry of Education's survey in 1962 of the stock of school buildings had shown that of the 3,873,200 children in primary schools some

666,000 were in schools built before 1875 and almost a million in schools built before 1902. The Labour Government's Circular 10/65 asked (it could not require) that local authorities should prepare schemes for the introduction of comprehensive systems of education and listed six possible options for the organization of secondary education which had been suggested to the Minister, Anthony Crosland, by HMI. There was no one form of comprehensive education advocated. Raymond King, the head of Wandsworth School, one of the outstandingly successful London comprehensives, had been at pains to pay tribute to the freedom given to its heads by the London County Council when he retired in 1964, referring to:

> the exciting variety of organizational pattern, both scholastic and social, in the London schools, and the immense range of experience they have collectively accumulated in the last ten years. (Quoted in Simon, 1985, p. 164)

The Labour Party's wholehearted commitment to comprehensive education had come relatively suddenly and the policy did not command total agreement among members. The circular marked the end of consensus on educational policy between the political parties and the attempts at its implementation aroused passionate feelings both for and against comprehensivization. When the Borough of Ealing in West London declared its intention of launching a pilot comprehensive scheme in Acton, for example, a committee of parents sought an injunction in the High Court to prevent it. They lost their case in July 1966, but the following April parents in Enfield, North London, served a High Court writ to prevent the reorganization of secondary education on comprehensive lines in the borough and, when they lost, appealed and received a delay in the implementation of the scheme. In the event, the effect of protest was minimal but the election of a Conservative Government from 1970 to 1974 led to the withdrawal of Circular 10/65 and on 21 March 1975 *The Times Educational Supplement* published a survey showing that only 20 of the 104 local authorities had all their secondary pupils in comprehensive schools and seven had declared that they had no intention of reorganizing. It took fifteen years from the date of the Circular and the Education Act of 1976, which gave the Secretary of State the power to require local authorities to submit proposals for comprehensive reorganization within five years, before comprehensive education became almost universal.

The control of central government

Until the Education Act of 1976 central government's power over the organization of secondary education was restricted to the approval (or disapproval) of proposals initiated by the local authorities. As late as 1977 D.E. Regan could write: 'Central government is a sleeping giant when it comes to running schools' (Regan, 1977, p. 37). On the other hand, as Dr Eric Briault, the former Director of Education for Inner London, has pointed out, the most characteristic feature of central government is its power to say 'no'. This may be by influence or by direction, perhaps by way of removal of resources. Middle schools afford an interesting example of the effects of central government's influence as such. The Education Act of 1964 allowed the establishment of middle schools; Circular 10/65 specifically stated that the creation of the schools for pupils aged 8 to 12 or 9 to 13 'has an immediate attraction in the context of secondary reorganization on comprehensive lines'; HMI in *Towards the Middle School* (1970) identified various approaches to the curriculum. But a decade later the Inspectorate came to frown upon the middle school as expensive and inefficient. For instance, in the report on HMI visits in 1979 and 1980 to 48 out of the 610 9–13 middle schools which existed in 1983, fewer than half the surveyed schools reached generally satisfactory standards in the curriculum and only five were held to have attained good standards (DES, 1983, p. 17). Secretaries of State, of course, have also exerted influence. Rates of progress on individual and social opportunity in education since the War have depended very much on the Secretary of State's willingness and ability to secure appropriate legislation and support from political party, from government, from Parliament. But in the classroom teachers have traditionally reigned supreme, other than when they have been subjected to a rare visit from the head or an inspector.

The greatest control central government possesses is the power of the purse. The provision of resources is more important than the promise of legislative clauses, as the failure to provide the county colleges envisaged by the 1944 Education Act demonstrates. Equally, the majority of the significant powers of local education authorities are enabling powers; the absence of centrally defined duties in relation to nursery, further and adult education and the measure of discretion allowed in such matters as the award of some student grants has enabled local authorities to develop widely differing patterns of provision. In fact the change in 1958 to a block grant, replaced in 1966 by the rate support grant, was among the first indications of central government concern over the increase in open-ended specific grants and the inflationary effects of such grants on public expenditure.

Local authorities and education

The combination of a breakdown in education consensus and of central government's determination to control education and other local government expenditure brought great pressure on local authority education committees in the late 1960s and 1970s. Under the Butler Act the education committees drew up to one-third of their members from outside their parent councils, which were becoming politically polarized. It is a measure of the increasing politicization of local government and hence of education that whereas in 1964 some 44 per cent of local authorities had just over half their membership composed of national party members, by 1973 the percentage had risen to 64. Although the reform of local government in 1972 left the statutory education committee and the appointment of a chief education officer intact the position of local authority education committees

49

was weakened by the campaign to remove such special protection for educational interests, by the increasing tendency in many authorities for effective decision-making to take place not in open council but in the majority party caucus meeting, and by the development of corporate management after the reorganization in 1974 which put education on a competitive footing with other local government departments for resources. In theory the concept of corporate management was intended to allow local authorities to decide how they would resource each of their services. In the outcome the measure of local independence which this allowed was in conflict with the strong central control over public expenditure, a concern of both Labour and Conservative governments. Equally, the removal of some government services, such as health and water, to appointed local bodies in 1974, indicated a reduced commitment by Parliament to the value of elected local government. The low turn-out of voters in local elections (approximately 40 per cent as against 70 per cent in a general election) evidently weighed more heavily with the politicians than the words of the Royal Commission on Local Government in 1969: 'If local self-government withers the roots of democracy grow dry. If it is genuinely alive, it nourishes the reality of democratic freedom.'

Central government, under the rate support grant system introduced in 1981, now decides the amount of total 'relevant expenditure' by local authorities for a given year. This is the figure held to be required for maintaining local authority services in accordance with government policies. The percentage of rate support fell from 71 in 1976–7 to 47.5 in 1986–7, a stupendous reduction which forced a concurrent rise in local rates.

The Treasury pressure to hold down public expenditure led the government to introduce a system of cash limits in the spring of 1976 and to suspend the voting of additional money to allow for inflation. The inability of central government to control spending in most areas of local government meant that the imposition of cash limits constituted a powerful but crude restriction on education spending. The effects have been twofold. First, local authorities have become deeply resentful of central government intervention, particularly of the application of a scale of penalties on local authorities who spend more than the suggested limit and of the imposition of 'rate capping' when that expenditure exceeds a specified limit. Secondly, the inability of local authorities to maintain the level of educational provision previously held to be necessary has demoralized the profession.

Jackson Hall, the former chief education officer for Sunderland, has put it this way:

> The education service is carried on in premises which are deteriorating because of inadequate maintenance and repair; the furniture stock is also deteriorating; the equipment is below par; the supply of textbooks is gravely deficient, and most libraries are inadequate. Too many schools have roofs that leak, rotting window frames, walls that require repointing, an electrical installation that requires replacement or up-grading, a heating system that should be replaced, and neglected paintwork. It is possible that inadequate maintenance of the physical stock of the service is costing as much as vandalism. (Hall, 1987, pp. 5–6)

Control over the curriculum

Central government has sought to control more than expenditure in the last twenty years. At the same time as the Ministry was reconstructed in 1964, the Schools Council for the Curriculum and Examinations was established. It became a major force for educational change, uniquely bringing together representatives of teachers and educational administrators, inspectors and examiners. It replaced the Secondary School Examinations Council, which had existed since 1917, and initiated innovative approaches to curriculum development, such as the Nuffield Humanities Project (from 1967) and a common system of examining at 16-plus (proposed in 1971). Although the Schools Council was criticized for paying too little attention in its earlier projects to local circumstances and initiatives, it was always conscious of the delicacy of its situation in relation to schools. In its Working Paper 53, *The Whole Curriculum 13–16*, it suggested that the aims of a school should be stated in a 'covenant' to which parents, pupils, teachers and society could subscribe:

> British schools have for long been jealous of their independence in curriculum matters. However much they may turn to outside bodies for resources, information and advice, they insist that the curriculum must be of their own making. We strongly affirm our support for this position ... the surest hope for the improvement of the secondary school curriculum lies in the continuing professional growth of the teachers. (1975, p. 30)

In many ways the Schools Council was a perfect example of partnership in education: financed jointly by the DES and the LEAS, it had a majority of teachers on all committees except the General Purposes Committee and from 1964 to 1973 an HMI as one of its joint secretaries. By statute, the Secretary of State has the power to approve school-leaving examinations and the local authority carries the ultimate responsibility for the curriculum, subject only to the statutory requirements for the inclusion of religious instruction, but in practice the curriculum has been the sphere of teacher power, subject only to general control by the managers or governors. In both primary and secondary schools, a fair degree of similarity exists in practice, although significant differences occur in the integration or separation of subjects at secondary level, in the allocation of time for particular subjects, and in the syllabuses of individual subjects. As Sheila Browne, Chief HMI, commented to a conference of local education authorities in July 1977:

> The present primary curriculum undoubtedly gives priority to the basic skills, firstly to language skills, in descending order reading, writing, and spoken word; and then to mathematics, with practice for the four rules taking precedence over investigation and practical work.

Or, as Maurice Kogan pointed out in 1975, looking at the issue from a managerial viewpoint, 30,000 educational institutions in England and Wales were free to develop their own organizational and educational styles.

Discontent with education

Serious reservations about the efficacy of the educational system and its ability to provide equality of opportunity became widespread. Anthony Crosland put it well in a tract for the Fabian Society in 1975:

> Where once we were sure that better education would enable working-class children to catch up with children of the middle classes, we know, thanks to the work of Jencks and his associates in the United States, that ... the character of a school's output depends largely on a single input, namely the character of entering children. Everything else — the school budget, its policies, the characteristics of the teachers — is either secondary or completely irrelevant. Moreover, we underestimated the capacity of the middle classes to use their political skills to appropriate more than their fair share of public expenditure.
> (Crosland, 1975, pp. 8–9)

Disillusionment with education's power to bring about change, concern over the cost of the educational system, loss of confidence in the Department of Education's efficiency, as illustrated by its miscalculations over the birthrate at the time of the White Paper ironically titled *A Framework for Expansion*, were now joined by public controversies over individual schools and by adverse assessment of the English educational service by outsiders. HMI had registered reservations about the concept of open-plan primary schools in a report in 1972. Some of the concerns then expressed were raised in an acute form by the case over William Tyndale primary school in North London where such conflict arose between teachers, parents, managers and the Inner London Education Authority that a public inquiry had to be held under Mr R. Auld, QC, who reported in 1976. The teachers, who adopted an admittedly extreme version of 'progressive' teaching, were subjected to heavy criticism and it was noticed that the local authority appeared to be unable to exert control. A team of inspectors were met with less than full co-operation and Harvey Hinds, the former chairman of the Schools Sub-Committee, told the inquiry:

In the English system, the attitude of the education authorities is one of leaving teachers to teach and managers to manage, relying on a mutual confidence which in experience is rarely shown not to exist.

(*The Times Educational Supplement*, 5 May 1975)

It happened that in May 1976, Neville Bennett and associates published a report on *Teaching Styles and Pupil Progress* which was widely publicized by the media in an over-simplistic way to suggest that traditional teaching tended to produce better results than progressive. The report's findings were much more sophisticated than this publicity suggested but it was the *perception* of what had been written which influenced public opinion.

The previous year the OECD produced a report by an American, a German and a Frenchman on the English educational system which criticized the DES for lack of planning and commented that the British planning process could be seen either as a set of paradoxes or as a subtle blend of mutually supporting virtues.

The Great Debate

The generally felt disillusion with the education system led to a lively concern with efficiency. This was manifested in the Prime Minister James Callaghan's speech at Ruskin College, Oxford in October 1976, in which he alluded to the widespread feeling that standards in many areas, including education, needed to rise but were not doing so, and called for a wide debate on educational issues. The Secretaries of State for England and Wales, after conferring with a large number of interested parties, organized eight regional conferences with the object of concentrating discussion on four main issues: the school curriculum, 5–16; the assessment of standards; the education and training of teachers; and the relationship between schools and working life. In July 1977 the Government presented a statement of its provisional views in a Green Paper, *Education in Schools*. This prepared the way for Circular 14/77, a quite unprecedented request to LEAS to review and report on fifty questions about

largely from the advanced further education pool, to which all local authorities contributed for the costs of colleges maintained by only some of them. Control was exerted locally by the education authority through a governing body and nationally by the Department of Education and Science through the requirement that public sector courses could be run only with the Secretary of State's approval, and through the reports of HMI. A great virtue of the binary system from the point of view of central government was its comparatively modest cost. The average expenditure per full-time student in non-autonomous colleges of further and higher education in 1964–5 was under £220 as against around £900 in universities and colleges of advanced technology. Inevitably the polytechnics suffered difficulties in offering balanced courses, in setting standards, in securing sufficient funding from local authorities, and had some poor publicity as a result of student militancy being concentrated in them during 1968. None the less, they established themselves as alternatives to the conventional universities in a remarkably short period of time.

An even greater success attended the Open University, which took its first students in 1971. Harold Wilson mooted the development in a speech in Glasgow in 1963 but it was Jennie Lee as Minister for the Arts who defined its purpose and carried the idea through against opposition in Parliament and in the Department of Education and Science. In his inaugural address as Chancellor, Lord Crowther in 1969 declared that the University — and it is significant that it was to rank as a completely independent university from the start — was to be open as to people, places, methods and ideas. There was to be no compromise on standards but entry was to be open to all without any restriction other than that of the availability of places. The Open University gave a second chance to those who for whatever reason had lost out on higher education at the usual age. It shortly established itself as the major institution of distance learning in the world. The work of its course teams of academics and media experts has produced programmes for radio and television of exceptional quality but, above all, correspondence course material which has been unquestionably of the highest standard in both content and presentation. Its publications can hold their own for value anywhere in the world and its costs amount to only a small fraction of ordinary university funding. Moreover, it has from the beginning set new standards of assessment and evaluation of its courses. In short, the Open University has been very much a success story of central government intervention in education — cheap and efficient, winning widespread support from a broad cross-section of the population even if, as always, the middle classes have taken more than their fair share of the resources and opportunities offered.

Except for the Open University, which is funded directly by the Department of Education and Science, universities derive most of their finance for both capital and running costs from public funds through the University Grants Committee. From 1968 university accounts have been open to public audit and the UGC came to exercise some direction despite the legal independence of universities. As the Committee put it in its *Annual Survey* for 1974–5:

> We consider it right...that we should exercise influence on the universities, and particularly on the shape of the system as a whole, so that...it corresponds to national needs. But we do not interpret this as meaning transmission of some plan conceived centrally.
>
> (UGC, *Annual Survey*, 1976, para. 7)

Members of the Committee were, after all, in large measure drawn from university staff. Like other sections of the education service, universities had to accept the cash limits on expenditure imposed in 1976. Their forward planning was thrown into disarray by the abandonment of the quinquennial system of grants. Previously, their income was known for a five-year period and there was a virtually automatic supplementation to provide for salary increases and for inflation. From the end of 1973, supplementation was suspended and the Exchequer grants paid through the UGC, which in 1974–5 constituted just over three-quarters of university funding (fees accounted for 4.5 per cent and endowment for 1.1 per cent), became in effect annual allocations. Even so, where in 1962 universities in the United Kingdom had had 113,000 full-time equivalent students, in 1978 they had 280,000. The Department of Education and Science's position in relation to the postgraduate work of universities was reinforced by the Science and Technology Act of 1965, which made it responsible for supporting the research councils and university-based scientific research.

Teacher training

Colleges of education remained in many ways the half-way house between the universities and the public sector; though the term 'binary system' was commonly used in the later 1960s, it would have been more appropriate to acknowledge the position of the colleges of education and speak of a 'trinary system'. The Robbins Report had recommended that the colleges should be administered by the universities but vested interests in local government secured the rejection of that recommendation, so they continued to be maintained by local authorities or voluntary bodies. As a result of the Weaver Report, every college of education had its own governing body (unlike the technical colleges) and through discussions and shared administration with university staff at the institutes of education staff took an active part in decisions on curriculum, examinations and validation. The move towards an all-graduate teaching profession, which was broadly acceptable as a desirable outcome of the Robbins proposals, was to be achieved by the gradual introduction of three- and four-year courses for B.Ed. degrees and of in-service programmes leading to B.Ed., but of course entry to these courses was determined not by the colleges but by the local university's senate. Between 1964 and 1972 the number of students in teacher training nearly doubled, from around 65,000 to around 120,000. Government came under increasing pressure to investigate teacher education in both the public and university sectors. In February 1970, Edward Short, the then Secretary of State, asked each area training organization to survey the courses for which it was responsible and when, later in the year, a Conservative government was elected, a committee of enquiry was established under Lord James of Rusholme. The James Report was quickly followed by the White Paper *Education: A Framework for Expansion* which proposed the abolition of the university-based area training organizations (generally called institutes of education) and the creation of new regional committees funded by the DES.

The James Report and the White Paper provoked much discussion of teacher training within and outside the profession. An important policy statement was made by the Universities Council for the Education of Teachers in May 1973, *The In-service Education and Training of Teachers*. The distinction, so long made in teacher training, between personal and professional development was rejected but the imperative need for a more broadly conceived and extended programme of in-service education for teachers was accepted. UCET advocated the provision of in-service education in 'the whole range of knowledge, theory and practice relevant to teachers as professional people' — and the profession has demonstrated in recent years a readiness to respond to such provision in excess of the action actually taken.

Though locally administered, the colleges of education were very much under the control of the Secretary of State from 1944 onwards, and the White Paper marked the beginning of a new emphasis on central government as the originator of policy in both initial and in-service teacher education. Section 62 of the Education Act of 1944 had laid the duty on the minister to secure 'sufficient facilities for the training of teachers ... and ... give to any local education authority such directions as he thinks necessary requiring them to establish, maintain, or assist any training college or other institution'.

Circular 7/73 from the DES called for LEA plans for the organization of teacher training; the Further Education Regulations of 1975 abolished the area training organization and incorporated the policy of the assimilation of teacher education, outside the universities, into a common system. Together, these powers gave the Secretary of State unique control and the ability to secure rapid adaptation to the needs of the system as perceived centrally. Government was not slow to use these powers and the resistance offered by both local authorities and the voluntary bodies was pathetically weak. An extensive programme of mergers and closures of teacher training institutions began. There is little doubt that HMI opinion was sought and their reports taken into account but there was no known connection between HMI inspections and closures, any more indeed than there was any obvious relation between quality and survival. The number of institutions fell from 196 in 1968 to 118 in 1979 and the number of students in training was reduced from around 120,000 in 1972 to around 55,000 in 1981. Despite the cuts in intake, only 57 per cent of students entering colleges of education in 1977 had two or more A levels. Concern over the calibre of teacher trainees and of teachers in service led to the stress in the Green Paper *Education in Schools* (1977) on the need for education authorities to develop more systematic approaches to the recruitment, training, deployment and career development of their teachers (DES, 1977a, para. 6, pp. 32–3). Shirley Williams as Secretary of State made money available for local authority induction programmes but, with honourable exceptions such as Northumberland, few authorities used the money as it was intended to be used. Further, in February 1978 it was laid down by the DES that all entrants to teaching from 1980 would be required to have O levels at grade C or above, or an equivalent qualification in English Language and Mathematics.

Further education

The Crowther Report in 1959 had spoken of the need to provide 'an alternative form of education for those who had got incurably tired of school and for those whose schools had no sixth form' (Ministry of Education, 1959, p. 412). The colleges of further education grew markedly in the 1960s. By 1966 they accounted for more than two-fifths of the entries at A level: a survey in the mid-1970s showed that students sought a more mature environment than was offered in schools as well as the wider choice of subjects provided by the colleges. Before 1964 the maintained system did little to train workers in industry and commerce, leaving that task to the companies. The Industrial Training Act established some twenty-one training boards under the Department of Employment to be responsible for the quality and quantity of training within a range of industries affecting 11 million workers. The boards were to make a levy on firms in their industry, proportionate to the size of the company's payroll; firms could claim back the costs of sending employees. The effect upon the colleges was dramatic. They needed to stay open for up to 48 weeks of the year and they developed, in close association with local industry and commerce, a range of courses combining further education and training in specific skills.

Vocational training came increasingly to the fore of governmental thinking in the 1970s. As Dean and Choppin pointed out, since the War there had been two clear and separate paths for those continuing their education beyond the school-leaving age. The products of the grammar schools had stayed on in the sixth forms and gone to universities and polytechnics while those of the secondary modern schools had joined the colleges of further education:

> There was little liaison between establishments in the two sectors. They operated under different regulations, were staffed by teachers with different backgrounds and saw their functions as being distinct and separate.
>
> (Dean and Choppin, 1977, p. 39)

In 1977 the Further Education Review and Development Unit was placed under the DES to collaborate in the development of courses of vocational preparation. Central government now accepted that it had largely to pay for and to secure national training provision. As a report of a seminar held at Dillington House, Somerset, in October 1977 put it:

> We can no longer concentrate on the 30–40 per cent who opt to continue in education or training at 16. We also have a duty to provide for those who opt out. They should not find the door closed to them for ever, as a penalty for making a wrong choice at 16.
>
> (Open University, 1979, Unit 12, p. 7)

The Manpower Services Commission was set up under the Department of Employment to cater for the training needs of this group; also, of course, to help meet the training needs of industry which were of special national priority. This initiative involved massively increased funding for educational purposes outside the usual agencies and represented a massive vote of no confidence in the education service. Industry would still provide the greater part of training but there would be an increasing number of government-backed courses and, in particular, unified vocational schemes for those in employment. From 1 April 1978 the Youth Opportunities Programme provided training also for those not in employment, perhaps 70 per cent of them in colleges of further education. This was central intervention with a vengeance.

Adult education

The general attitude of central and local government to adult education has been one of extraordinary neglect. Grants from the DES are made under the Further Education Regulations to the Workers' Educational Association and the University Departments of Extra-Mural Studies (now often called Departments of Adult and Continuing Education), but when the Russell Committee reported on adult education in 1973 it was more than fifty years since there had been a similar review, and the report was concerned to establish a secure place for adult education in the maintained system. Its definition of adult education makes this clear:

> opportunities for men and women to continue to develop their knowledge, skills, judgement and creativity throughout adult life by taking part, from time to time, in learning situations which have been set up for the purpose as *part of the total public provision of education* [italics added].

(DES, 1973, para. 8)

The Council of Europe report, *Permanent Education*, published in the same year, recognized that education in a complex and changing world could no longer be equated with schooling but must be a continuing process throughout life and, equally, that schooling could no longer be equated with the acquisition of knowledge:

> The schooling of youth will be less and less a matter of acquiring knowledge (soon outdated) and information (provided more comprehensively elsewhere) but will be more and more devoted to the acquisition of methods of thought, adaptive attitudes, critical reactions, and disciplines which teach how to learn.
>
> (Council of Europe, 1973, p. 22)

However, although adult education was recognized as important the Russell Report had rather depressing news to impart on progress in England and Wales:

> Such initiatives as have come from the Ministry of Education and its successor the Department of Education and Science have had a significant effect on local authorities: for example, the growth in the number of full-time appointments since 1963 shows with what seriousness the Administrative Memorandum no. 6 of that year was acted upon. Unfortunately the other circulars and memoranda ... have usually had the raising of fees as their primary concern.
>
> (DES, 1973, para. 155)

Adult education provision remained a matter of discretion for the local education authorities. Most provided the kind of courses traditionally associated with 'night school' in vocational or hobby subjects but many were less than fully committed to adult education as became apparent when in 1968 a few authorities decided to abandon it entirely as an economy measure. The Inner London Education Authority was a notable exception and maintained the worthy tradition of London in providing the whole range of adult education.

There was, however, one area in which the Department of Education and Science was prepared to take a firm initiative — adult literacy. The Adult Literacy Resource Agency was established in April 1975 to assist local authorities and voluntary bodies to tackle the problem of adult illiteracy which had come to be a matter of public concern. Evidence presented in the Bullock

Report, *A Language for Life* (1975), suggested that standards of literacy had fallen, though the Committee rightly drew attention to the difficulty of definition. *Black Paper 1975* argued that the best way to help children in deprived areas was to help them become literate and numerate and persuaded Sir Cyril Burt to demonstrate, from figures which have subsequently been questioned, that standards had in fact fallen. In 1970 about half of all local authorities made provision for literacy programmes; in 1978 many others were persuaded to do so by including some £1,300,000 in the Rate Support Grant for basic literacy education.

Minority groups

Central government was not always so decisive, as may be illustrated from another area of public concern — the education of immigrant children and of the children of immigrants. The Commonwealth Immigrants Advisory Council in its report in 1964 argued:

> A national system of education must aim at producing citizens who can take their place in society properly equipped to exercise rights and perform duties which are the same as other citizens. If their parents were brought up in another culture or another tradition, children should be encouraged to respect it, but a national system cannot be expected to perpetuate the different values of immigrant groups.
> (Commonwealth Immigrants Advisory Council, 1964, p. 7)

Circular 7/65 incorporated this philosophy, referring to the task of education as 'the successful assimilation of immigrant children' and stressing the importance of the acquisition of English. Roy Jenkins, Home Secretary in 1966, declared that such assimilation was to be 'equal opportunity accompanied by cultural diversity, in an atmosphere of tolerance' (Hiro, 1971, p. 355). There was indeed a shift of emphasis in the later 1960s and 1970s in some English schools towards a more positive concept of 'multi-cultural education', accompanied by an increased awareness of the real enrichment which the children of ethnic minorities could bring to the life of a school. Apart from Circular 7/65, however, central government carefully avoided the formulation of prescribed policy on the issue and the chief education officers reported to the Community Relations Commission in 1976:

> Little attempt appears to have been made either to formulate a national policy in other than the most general terms or to estimate the cost of an adequate ethnic minority education programme.
>
> (Community Relations Council, 1976, p. 6)

Public opinion was mercifully in advance of public policy in the period and there has been a steadily enhanced awareness of the inequalities in British society and in educational provision, whether it be in relation to ethnic minorities, to class differentiation or to gender discrimination. Just how great a need there was for this awareness had been highlighted by the Robbins Committee in 1963 when it reported:

> The proportion of young people who enter full-time higher education is 45 per cent for those whose fathers are in the 'higher professional' groups, compared with only 4 per cent for those whose fathers are in skilled manual occupations ... The link is even more marked for girls than for boys.
>
> (Ministry of Education, 1963, vol. 1, p. 51)

The Hadow Report on the primary school in 1931 had been concerned to argue that while girls were doing needlework, boys should be occupied with activities likely to appeal to them especially, such as scale drawing, surveying or handicraft. The HMI Primary Survey of 1978 reflected a changed attitude:

> There is no justification for differentiation between the curriculum for boys and for girls because of traditional differences in social roles; such differentiation as does still occur, for example in craft work which limits girls to using soft materials, is unusual and should cease.
>
> (DES, 1978, para. 8.29)

HMI are rarely so prescriptive in their comments; here they clearly felt that public opinion was quite opposed to gender differentiation in the curriculum.

The independent schools

The Labour Government naturally had severe reservations about the continued existence of independent schools but what is most remarkable is how little debate occurred in the 1960s and 1970s on the issue and how much less action was actually taken. The reports of the Public Schools Commission in 1968 (on public schools) and 1970 (on independent day schools and direct grant schools) produced little stirring of the waters of public controversy. The first report explained that in the post-war period public schools:

> have been changing their assumptions and aims, diversifying and opening up their culture. The change of emphasis to academic achievement, a decline in the importance of team games, a greater concern for the arts, and some dismantling of the complex disciplinary machine, are all, in many schools, conspicuous. Nevertheless … their activities are based on the assumptions and aspirations of the British middle class.
>
> (Public Schools Commission, *First Report*, 1968, vol. I, p. 18)

They were held to be a 'divisive influence in society', as well they might be in the sense that a disproportionate percentage of top posts were filled from their products. In 1956, for instance, 76 per cent of judges and in 1964, 35 per cent of the Labour Government's Cabinet came from public schools (Glennerster and Pryke, 1964, p. 17). Like the Fleming Committee before it, the Commission sought an integration of the independent and maintained school sectors, by making more than half the places in independent schools available to pupils from maintained schools, chosen for their ability or for their 'boarding need'. 'Boarding need' was a concept popularized, indeed, by the Commission — it embraced the social need of children from adverse home or family conditions and the academic need of children of special ability who could not obtain an appropriate education locally. The Commission recommended the creation of a Boarding Schools Corporation to oversee schemes for the greater integration of the sectors and advised that a small number

69

of schools should become sixth form colleges and a few cater for aptitude in such specializations as music or the ballet. Most independent schools possess charitable status and are therefore exempt from paying some taxes, including VAT, and are able to claim mandatory rate relief of 50 per cent. The majority of the Public Schools Commission felt that there was no case for what amounts to a general subsidy for private education and recommended the withdrawal of these facilities.

The second report recommended that direct grant and independent day schools should become comprehensive schools, financed through a School Grants Committee. After 31 December 1975, the Labour Government withdrew the unit grants per child paid to Direct Grant schools by the DES for children entering the schools, in effect abolishing the system of Direct Grant schools. Most (119 out of 174) such schools subsequently opted for full independent status; four closed and the others became voluntary aided comprehensive schools.

The action over Direct Grant schools was virtually all that was done to implement the recommendations of the Public Schools Commission. This is not surprising, as both local authorities and central government use the independent schools extensively. Although little notice was taken of the Commission's definition of 'boarding need' or of the much fuller statement which resulted from Dr Royston Lambert's study *The Chance of a Lifetime?* (1975), local education authorities have given assistance to children with special needs, as in the provision of education for the subnormal or maladjusted. The Secretary of State's approval for such schemes has to be given; the cost in 1976–7 was £23 million. The Ministry of Defence and the Foreign Office spend large sums every year on the education in independent schools of the children of members of the armed forces and the Diplomatic Service (in 1976–7, £36 million).

Far from being weakened in the late 1960s and 1970s, the independent schools flourished. The attempt to integrate Direct Grant schools worked in their favour, leading to an increase in pupil numbers. They remained as a source of vital support for the maintained system, especially in specialist areas and in the provision of boarding facilities, and were, despite the rise in their fees because of inflation, increasingly popular with parents who could afford to use them, as confidence in the comprehensive system declined. In short, the independent schools demonstrate the efficacy of public, and especially middle-class, opinion as a control in education in our democracy. As Harold Silver has put it, '(Sir Fred) Clarke has been proved wrong in assuming that a convincing sociology plus a determined restructuring of the secondary school would alone make major inroads into the problems of a divided and unequal society' (Silver, 1980, p. 11).

4 Educational development in an age of centralization, 1979–88

The coming of Thatcherism

The election of a Conservative government in May 1979 has been widely held to mark a watershed in English educational development and to herald a new approach characterized by entrepreneurialism and centralization. This was not the view of Kenneth Baker, who explained in 1987 when putting forward his Education Reform Bill that 'far from seeking to destroy the traditional partnership between local education authorities and central government the legislative programme sought to build on its strengths by adding parents, employers and local communities' (*Education*, 24 July 1987).

The truth is, however, that the late 1970s saw a number of developments leading to increased centralization in educational provision in England and Wales as in other countries of the Western world. Dudley Fiske, the chief education officer for Manchester, listed five of the factors making for reduced local government influence in his presidential address to the Society of Education Officers in January 1978 (*Education*, 27 January 1978). He drew attention to the increased impact of party politics, holding the 1974 local government re-organization to have 'marked the final decline on education authorities of the elected member who was genuinely independent'; the popular faith in the value for restructuring educational and local government systems as an aid to progress; the greater participation in decision-making of 'consumers', students as well as parents; the introduction of protective legislation such as the Sex

Discrimination Act of 1975; and the contraction in local educational provision resulting from final cutbacks, falling rolls, and rising unemployment.

The Green Paper *Education in Schools* (1977) had acknowledged the tendency to blame the education service for the ills of society over which it could have no control: 'Some genuine anxieties should be directed elsewhere than at our schools; they have been made scapegoats for other pressures and forces working in society' (DES, 1977a, p. 39). But many felt at the time that the government actually exploited the demand for the accountability of the education service (which had been carefully promoted by the Department of Education and Science), and subscribed to the view that teachers and schools had failed young people. The partnership approach was collapsing; as Eric Briault, a former chief education officer for ILEA, has pointed out, a better metaphor was a triangle of tension between the DES, LEAs and teachers, held together by a common concern but pulled apart by conflicting viewpoints and differing priorities for resources. Anthony Crosland, Secretary of State 1965–7, could comment, 'The nearer one comes to the professional content of education, the more indirect the Minister's influence is' (Kogan, 1971, p. 135), and no mention of the curriculum was made in the White Paper *Education: A Framework for Expansion* (1972), it being understood that central government was content to address itself to the provision of improved material conditions for schooling. By contrast, by the late 1970s, the Permanent Secretary to the Department of Education and Science was declaring: 'The key to the secret garden of the curriculum has to be found and turned' (Fenwick and McBride, 1981, p. 220).

A new attitude prevailed and the call was for more control from the centre. An HMI Working Paper on the *Curriculum 11–16* of 1977, known as Red Book One, epitomized the mood:

> It is doubtful if the country can afford — educationally as well as financially — the wasted effort, the experiments embarked upon and left unfinished or unexamined, unnecessary repetitions, and, most of all, the apparent lack of agreement on fundamental objectives.
>
> (Quoted in Fowler, 1988, pp. 42–3)

73

HMI put forward for discussion eight essential 'areas of experience': the aesthetic and creative; the ethical; the linguistic; the mathematical; the physical; the scientific; the social and political; and the spiritual. In 1977 the DES had asked local authorities to report on their curriculum policies and the *Report on 14/77 Review* (1979) indicated, just as Mrs Thatcher's government took office, that some LEAS had no satisfactory curriculum policy at all:

> The Secretaries of State believe that they should give a lead in the process of reaching a national consensus on a desirable framework for the curriculum. (DES, 1979)

The discontent was not confined to the content of the curriculum; there was also concern over the quality of teaching methodology. The HMI survey of comprehensive schools in 1978, for instance, singled out the use of worksheets:

> While we found ... mixed ability grouping, we had greater difficulty in finding mixed ability teaching ... many of the examples (of worksheets) seen failed to provide differentiation, confused pace of working with level of work ... and did not offer problem-solving opportunities. (Quoted in Fowler, 1988, p. 53)

Early signs of centralism 1980–81

The new government lost no time in introducing legislation and in producing documents expounding its educational thinking. The 1980 Education Act was expressly designed to control local expenditure and to give parents more power. Thus local authorities no longer had to provide school meals or milk except for pupils from families on Family Income Supplement or Supplementary Benefit, and the provision of nursery education was made discretionary. The differences between the governing bodies of primary and secondary schools were abolished and two elected parent representatives were to be on the governing bodies of all maintained schools. The Act detailed regulations on the provision of information by schools, including the publication of examination results by secondary schools. Another section of the

Act allowed for up to 15,000 'assisted places', funded directly by the DES each year at independent schools to provide for the rich in talent who were poor financially. This was one of the Act's most controversial features and some local authorities have instructed heads not to supply references for pupils in their schools who seek to take advantage of the provision.

A trilogy of documents was published on the curriculum: a DES consultative paper *A Framework for the School Curriculum* (January 1980), an HMI 'Matters for Discussion' publication *A View of the Curriculum* (1980), and a DES document *The School Curriculum* (March 1981). The consultative paper aroused some hostility; it would seem HMI had not been adequately consulted. It called for each local authority to have 'clear and known policies for the curriculum' and to plan future developments in consultation with teachers. It declared it timely to propose a core curriculum to 'ensure that all pupils ... at least get a sufficient grounding in the knowledge and skills which by common consent should form part of the equipment of the educated adult' (quoted in Fowler, 1988, p. 59).

It further, and most significantly, proposed specific amounts of time for each of the common core elements.

A View of the Curriculum appealed to teachers and educationalists rather more, making the point that a common core curriculum would have to be accompanied by curricular programmes catering for the individual needs of pupils. In admitting the absence of an imposed curriculum in English secondary schools, it acknowledged that:

> habit and common sense ensure that schools, in practice, are not so divergent as the lack of any explicit common curriculum policy might suggest. Nevertheless, there are sufficient grounds for unease to suggest a need to re-examine the rationale and organisational structure of the prevailing curriculum in many secondary schools.
>
> (HMI, 1980)

The third document, *The School Curriculum*, a revised version of *Framework*, took account of the discussion which had taken place and showed a greater readiness to recognize that much good work already took place in schools: 'What is now needed is to develop a good deal of what is common practice in a more demanding way.' The call for a common curriculum was reiterated and secondary schools were particularly urged to plan their curricula as a whole. Of course, as Professor Denis Lawton has emphasized:

> The existence of national guidelines on the school curriculum is not necessarily in conflict with the idea of professional autonomy: an individual teacher can still exercise professional judgement about *exactly* what to teach (and when) provided that the national (or regional) prescriptions are not set out in the form of detailed syllabuses or lesson plans. (Lawton, 1984, p. 15)

But to most teachers the proposal smacked of centralized control and appeared to be a threat to their independence.

The 1981 Education Act

The Conservative government was not slow either to embody some of the recommendations of the Warnock Report of 1978 in its Education Act of 1981. The committee established under Mrs Mary Warnock had been charged 'to review educational provision for children and young people handicapped by disabilities of body and mind'. The resulting Report was at pains to stress the continuum between the handicapped and the rest of the population but called for the provision of protected resources for the small minority of children with severe and complex special needs as identified by formal, multi-disciplinary assessment and 'statementing' — i.e. the provision of a formal statement of the special educational needs of children in special schools or units and those in ordinary schools who have such learning difficulties that they require extra resources. The Act led to a marked increase in support services such as educational psychological services. However, these may have been developed by local authorities as an alternative to properly resourcing ordinary schools to accommodate children with special educational needs, which is what the Act required of local authorities except where such integration would be incompatible with the children receiving appropriate educational provision or the efficient education of the other children in the school, or the efficient use of the authority's resources. Nevertheless, the Warnock Report alerted the public as well as the profession to the widespread nature of learning difficulties and the imperative need for the provision of greater resources to remedy those difficulties in the interests of society as well as of the individuals concerned.

The 1981 Act also affected parents' rights and duties, stressing the famous section 76 of the 1944 Act which stated 'pupils are to be educated in accordance with the wishes of their parents' as far as possible and including further provision for parents to make their views known, to be involved in assessments, and to receive information.

Curriculum initiatives 1982–3

A curriculum suitable for the majority of pupils continued to exercise the minds of HMI. At primary level, there was the question of how to make the best use of the curriculum strengths of teachers, how to achieve the right balance between class teaching and the input of teachers' specialist expertise. The HMI Report *Education 5–9: An Illustrative Study by HMI* found, for example, that too often the role of specialist mathematics teachers was limited to 'the production of guidelines or checklists or even, as with the equally important area of language, solely to the provision and organization of teaching material' (HMI, 1982, para. 3.21).

From 1979 onwards five LEAS and 41 schools had been contributing to a joint curricular enquiry monitored by the DES, which resulted in *Curriculum 11–16: Towards a Statement of Entitlement* (1983), familiarly known as Red Book Three. Its central issue was summarized in these words:

> The conviction has grown that all pupils are entitled to a broad compulsory common curriculum to the age of sixteen, which introduces them to a range of experience, makes them aware of the kind of society in which they are going to live and gives them the skills necssary to live in it ... Given the wide nature of the curriculum,

it is unlikely that its common elements can be achieved in less than 75 per cent of the time available in all of the five years of secondary schooling 11 to 16. (DES, 1983, ch. 3)

Since January 1983 reports following formal inspections of schools by HMI have been available for public scrutiny and they frequently contain references to curricular issues. The debate was well and truly engaged, therefore, but there was another major curriculum initiative from outside the Department of Education and Science which was launched in 1982 — the Technical and Vocational Education Initiative.

TVEI

The decision to place the Technical and Vocational Education Initiative under the Manpower Services Commission and not under the Department of Education and Science was without doubt a vote of no confidence in the education service. The government seemed to be implying that the education system had contributed to the massive increase in youth unemployment (unemployment among 16- and 17-year-olds had increased by 120 per cent between 1972 and 1977, for example, compared with a rise of 45 per cent in the population as a whole) because teachers had inculcated a negative attitude to business and industry. The truth was that, as Tony Watts pointed out, 'unemployment is a problem for education and not a result of education' (Watts, 1983, p. 20). The traditional compliance of children to school demands was based on an understanding which no longer applied: that industrious work in school would be rewarded with a job.

In November 1982 the MSC was invited to establish a number of pilot projects to develop successful teaching strategies for a technical and vocational education for 14- to 18-year-olds which could be applied to localities not initially involved. A National Steering Group was established drawing representatives from education, industry, commerce and local authorities and assessors from government departments. Within five years, 85 per cent of local authorities in the United Kingdom entered into TVEI contracts which involved loss of political control, something which they only accepted because of the injection of considerable additional resources. Thus the government, by giving money directly to the MSC for specific curriculum objectives, overcame the uncertainty of a decentralized system. Money given by the Treasury to the DES and on to the LEAs did not necessarily get spent on the curriculum change the government desired, however, or indeed on any curriculum change. The trend was strengthened with the announcement in the White Paper *Training for Jobs* (1983) that some money previously made available to LEAs for non-advanced further education was being directed to the MSC.

In most schools the TVEI element has run alongside conventional curriculum patterns for 14- to 16-year-olds and only been expected to comprise most of the curriculum after the age of 16. In 1984 only 18 per cent of 16-year-olds in Britain as a whole entered employment compared with 60 per cent ten years earlier, and there is no doubt that TVEI offered teachers an opportunity to bolster their own sense of purpose and to secure a greater pupil compliance by placing less emphasis on the value of qualifications and more on the direct relevance of school learning to employment. Some teachers believe that TVEI holds the potential for significant educational reform, for a pedagogy of experiential learning and problem-solving in a real as against an academic context. For it to work, however, there must be a sufficient number of appropriately qualified teachers in areas such as craft, design and technology, and information technology. Concern has been expressed by HMI that this is not the case. Further concern has been expressed by educational commentators, for example Harvey Wyatt, that a centralized initiative of this kind constitutes 'a threat to the educational values of comprehensive education' and that since able pupils are in practice kept away from TVEI programmes 'we will return to a school system that divides its pupils into sheep and goats at 14+ rather than at 11+' (Wyatt, 1985, p. 74). Furthermore, it was reported in *The Times Educational Supplement* of 1 July 1988 that the Training Commission (as the Manpower Services Commission had been renamed to recognize a changed emphasis) admitted to having no evidence that TVEI actually produces better qualified school-leavers — this, too, despite the introduction in 1984 of the Certificate in Pre-Vocational Education, examined by pupil profiling rather than by three-hour papers. CPVE was designed to provide a broad educational foundation for young people with few, if any, academic qualifications and has been used mainly by 17-year-olds who do not wish to commit themselves to an A-level course or to any particular occupation.

On the other hand, there is no denying that 'desirable attitudes to work are much less likely to be influenced by formal didactic teaching than by experiences, particularly where the experiences are reinforced by the peer-group because they have been involved in them' (Jamieson et al., 1988, p. 4), or that the further moves in the direction of TVEI in-service training (TRIST) and the School Curriculum Industry Partnership (SCIP) can only do good for the teaching profession and for education in general in strengthening the links between schools and industry. In 1987 the government announced the expansion of TVEI to 16- to 18-year-olds, a further testimony of its support for the development. Professor Richard Pring has gone so far as to state that TVEI has acted as a catalyst 'within a system which for too long has been captivated by a narrowing and inadequate notion of liberal education' (Pring, 1985, p. 15). The influence of TVEI has been very widespread: in 1986 there were 103 TVEI projects in 98 local authorities. The theory at least is attractive, as witness the description of TVEI in *Better Schools*:

> The TVEI embodies the Government's policy that education should better equip young people for working life. The courses are designed to cater equally for boys and girls across the whole ability range and with technical or vocational aspirations, and to offer in the compulsory years a broad general education with a strong technical element followed, post-16, by increasing vocational specialization. The course content and teaching methods adopted are intended to develop personal qualities and positive attitudes towards work as well as a wide range of competence, and more generally to develop a practical approach throughout the curriculum.
>
> (DES, 1985a, pp. 16–17)

Governmental intervention 1984–5

Sir Keith Joseph became Secretary of State for Education in September 1981. By the time he delivered the customary address from the Minister to the North of England Conference in January 1984, he had resolved upon an interventionist approach. In his address he proposed:

> To define the objectives of the main parts of the 5–16 curriculum so as to define the level of attainment which should be achieved at various stages by pupils of different abilities. To alter the 16+ examinations so that they would measure absolute rather than relative performance.

> To aim at bringing 80 to 90 per cent of all pupils at 16+ *at least* to the level currently achieved by pupils of average ability.

It was the programme of a visionary, designed to remove boredom from the secondary curriculum, to test children on what they could do and understand rather than to mark them down on what they did not know, and to relate schooling to the realities of the world of work. The major tool of the reform was to be the General Certificate of Secondary Education (GCSE), providing examinations to replace, from 1988, the O-level, CSE and joint 16-plus examinations. The Schools Council, which had initiated so much curriculum innovation from 1964, was abolished in favour of a Secondary Examinations Council (SEC) and a School Curriculum Development Committee. As an ex-HMI, W.S. Fowler, has put it: 'Beleaguered, badgered and branded by the DES as mediocre in performance, it certainly had no future in the face of the signals of centralism' (Fowler, 1988, p. 73). The Secondary Examinations Council consisted of the Secretary of State's appointees and had no formal representation from the teachers' unions. The School Curriculum Development Committee was established later and financed less generously. Thus curriculum development was made less influential than examination development and the balance of power was weighted against teachers and towards central government.

The O-level and CSE examining boards were restructured into five Examining Groups. Syllabuses and examinations were to be based on 'national criteria' developed over some years by committees of teachers, examiners and others and finally agreed by the Secondary Examinations Council and the Joint Council of GCE and CSE boards before publication by the Secretary of State in January 1985. The criteria consist of general guidelines for the examination as a whole (the General Criteria) and subject-specific guidelines (the National Criteria) for seventy selected subjects, which seek to reflect good practice. In general there is an increased emphasis on the assessment of candidates' work and skills, especially coursework, by their teachers and on differentiation by papers or questions or outcome. An extensive programme of in-service training was devised as well it needed to be, with a three-phase 'cascade' timetable. For GCSE marked a radical departure from long-established practice:

> where it could be argued that many candidates achieve their marks by relative failure at tasks and where, as a result, they may complete successfully only a small part of the paper. The result is that the examination is often a very unrewarding experience for many candidates. (SEC, *News* no. 1, Autumn 1985)

A White Paper, *Better Schools*, was published in March 1985. It embodied the ideas put forward by Sir Keith in 1984 at the North of England Conference and made clear that the twin aims of the government were to raise the standard of schooling at all levels of ability and to secure the best possible return from the resources invested in education. Chapter 2 defined the purposes of learning at school:

1. To help pupils to develop lively, enquiring minds, the ability to question and argue rationally and to apply themselves to tasks and physical skills;
2. To help pupils to acquire understanding, knowledge and skills relevant to adult life and employment in a fast-changing world;
3. To help pupils to use language and numbers effectively;
4. To help pupils to develop personal moral values, respect for religious values, and tolerance of other races, religions, and ways of life;

5. To help pupils to understand the world in which they live, and the inter-dependence of individuals, groups and nations;
6. To help pupils to appreciate human achievements and aspirations. (DES, 1985a, ch. 2)

There was a decidedly utilitarian purpose expressed in paragraph 9:

> Education at school should promote enterprise and adaptability in order to increase young people's chances of finding employment or creating it for themselves.

The White Paper embodied supremely the aspirations of the politicians with their concern for standards; of the officials of the DES with their advocacy of specific objectives; and of HMI with their support for a common curriculum. HMI's influence was very clear in the discussion of the curriculum, with its call for four fundamental principles — breadth, balance, relevance and differentiation — to be incorporated in any curriculum and for improved teacher training to reflect new approaches. Paragraph 162, for instance, read:

> Each new primary school teacher should be equipped to take a particular responsibility for one aspect of the curriculum ... to act as a consultant to colleagues on that aspect, and to teach it to classes other than his own.

Better Schools came to be one of the most widely quoted educational publications of the 1980s and for the most part it was quoted with approval. It distilled the thinking of some years, after all, and for the most part was uncontroversial. It was followed by the very practical HMI 'Curriculum Matters' pamphlet, *The Curriculum from 5–16*, which discussed central professional issues and argued that curriculum design and implementation must encompass 'areas of learning' (as previously defined but now with the addition of technological experience) and 'elements of learning' — knowledge, skill acquisition, and attitudes.

Paragraph 11 offered an all-encompassing definition of the curriculum which it declared:

> includes not only the formal programme of lessons, but also the 'informal' programmes of so-called extra-curricular activities as well

as all those features which produce the school's 'ethos', such as the quality of relationships, the concern for equality of opportunity, the values exemplified in the way the school sets about its task and the way in which it is organized and managed. (HMI, 1985, para. 11)

The paper concluded with a significant section on pupil assessment which argued that 'assessment is inseparable from the teaching process' and that 'pupils do not need to wait for a report to learn how they are progressing. The learning targets and progress towards achieving them are shared between teacher and pupil.'

Better Schools contained a statement which presaged the closure of a number of village schools in the succeeding years. Consistent with its advocacy of a curriculum-led rationale for schools, it contended that for a school to be educationally sound, except in some isolated communities, 'the number of pupils should not in general fall below the level at which a complement of three teachers is justified' (DES, 1985a, para. 175).

It was a cruel blow for many rural communities but of course made relatively little stir in an urban-dominated society.

The same cannot be said of the proposals revealed by Sir Keith Joseph at the North of England Conference on 4 January 1985, which affected every teacher in the land and moved the unions deeply. A prolonged teachers' strike followed. He argued for a full-scale appraisal system:

> The employing authority can only be satisfied that each school is properly staffed if it knows enough about the skills and competencies of individual teachers. Such knowledge can only come from some form of appraisal system. An appraisal system is also needed for the professional enhancement of the individual teacher.

He went on to acknowledge that such a system would need to be complemented by improved support for teachers including induction, in-service training, and career guidance. It was a clear demand for the application of management techniques to the teaching profession, as *The Times* diagnosed on 19 March 1985:

> At the heart of the teachers' dispute is not money but management. This dispute is about resistance to change in working practices ... By resisting the discipline of assessment of their own performance, the

teachers stand opposed to the renovation of Britain. That is why in this dispute management must win.

It did — with a heavy loss of teachers' morale and of public confidence in the profession.

The new structure of education 1986

By 1985 it was evident that there was a line management policy in the education service of England and Wales from the Cabinet to the humblest classroom. What was not evident was which of the Secretaries of State, for Education or for Employment, was managing director, since the main source of funds for curriculum development in the 1980s had been provided through the MSC.

In 1983 the DES had issued Circular 8/83, requiring local authorities to report on their curriculum policies, and the responses, which were made public in June 1986, showed how very variable these were. The 1986 Education Act received the Royal Assent in November and was designed to strengthen the role of the 'consumers' in curriculum development. Section 17 laid down that it was the duty of the local education authority to make, and keep up to date, a written statement of its policy in relation to the secular curriculum. Section 18 established it as the duty of governors to consider the authority's policy in relation to the secular curriculum in the light of the individual school's circumstances and to consider separately whether and how sex education should form part of the school's curriculum. Additionally, and it is a matter of historic importance, section 47 abolished corporal punishment in maintained schools from 1 August 1987. The Act, then, constricted the freedom of local authorities and increased the powers of governing bodies which were made more representative of parents and of the community; local authority representatives were to be always in a minority.

HMI's annual reports on the effects of local authority expenditure policies on education provision became public from 1984 and the 1985 annual report noted interestingly:

> There is a statistically significant association between satisfactory or better levels of appropriate resources and work of sound quality, and between unsatisfactory levels of resources and poor quality work.
>
> (Quoted in Fowler, 1988, p. 94)

Moreover, it found that disparities in provision both between and within local authorities and institutions were increasing. There was a clear message that national policies on curriculum development and plans for improved achievements could not be carried out without more, and more equally allocated, resources.

Meanwhile, the attack on the teaching profession continued from various quarters. The Hillgate Group, for instance, which consisted of such right-wing educationalists as Roger Scruton, Lawrence Norcross and Caroline Cox, produced a pamphlet, *Whose Schools? A Radical Manifesto*, which opened with the contention:

> [Parents] no longer have confidence that their children will acquire the learning and skills which will prepare them for membership of society. They have less and less assurance that moral standards, religious understanding and a respect for British institutions will be communicated to their children. (Quicke, 1988, p. 5)

1986 also saw the announcement of two reforms in the examination of 16- to 18-year-olds. The Secondary Examinations Council announced new guidelines for 1987 for A-level grading, revising those originally proposed in 1960. The principal alteration was to provide for a larger number of candidates to gain a C grade and fewer to be awarded E and N (or the former O-level equivalent). Under the previous system of grading, there was an unacceptably narrow group of candidates attaining grade C; in some instances, as few as 3 percentage points separated those gaining the minimum score for grade B from those gaining the highest score for grade D. Also a new examination course was announced as from September 1987, with the first examinations to be held in 1989 — AS level. The Advanced Supplementary Level courses were planned to broaden studies by offering an intermediary level between O and A, not by any lowering of standards but by restriction of curriculum. Students would be encouraged to take one or more AS levels in addition to, or more usually instead of one of, their A levels — perhaps a contrasting subject as, say, English for science students or mathematics for humanities students, or as a complementary subject as, say, design and technology for science students.

The superstructure of education 1987–8

By the North of England Education Conference of January 1987, Kenneth Baker had succeeded Sir Keith Joseph as Secretary of State. The thrust to central control was strengthened. The new Minister expatiated on the emptiness of the catchphrase 'a national system locally administered' and went so far as to dub the education system 'maverick' for want of a clear management structure. He referred to widespread concern over standards:

> If you look at examination results over the last ten years there is an improvement in the proportion of school-leavers with five or more higher grades in O level or CSE and there has been a small improvement in the proportion of those with two or more A levels, rising from 16 to 17 per cent. But when you consider the other changes in society over the last ten years, for example the greater involvement of girls in the education process, particularly in the sciences, and the huge increase in the resources per pupil, an increase of over 10 per cent in real terms, and the constant fall in the pupil–teacher ratio, one should expect very considerable improvements in standards.

He also made an unconcealed attack on local authorities, holding that their powers, if reduced by recent measures, remained substantial. 'I would be more concerned about LEAS losing functions if in general they had consistently made good use of their armoury of powers.' With visions of visits to certain London boroughs probably appearing before him as he spoke, he contended: 'LEAS cannot, in my view, apply to their functions a particular ideology to the point where educational effort becomes so disturbed that the pupils and students have a raw deal.' This was a gauntlet thrown down to those left-wing authorities which regarded the schools as political arenas for such policies as anti-racism and anti-sexism and the conflict was now clearly becoming a constitutional issue.

With the return of a third Conservative ministry in the summer of 1987, the Queen's Speech included an announcement of a Great Education Reform Bill and the Prime Minister was reported in July as hailing it as 'the key to the future' (*Independent*, 17 July 1987). With only nominal consultation, the Bill was published on 20 November and by the North of England Conference at Nottingham on 6 January 1988 the Minister was able to defend it on ideological grounds:

> It is about enhancing the life chances of young people. It is about the devolution of authority and responsibility. It is about competition, choice and freedom ... It is about quality and standards ... It is not about enhancing central control ... So far as financial delegation is concerned, the purpose of the legislation is to ensure that responsibility is shifted — not from local authorities to the centre — but from local authorities to the individual colleges and schools. It is thus a devolutionary and not a centralising measure.

The Education Act, 1988

The changes effected by the Act in the management of schools are far-reaching. The idea of decisions being taken at the point where they take effect is attractive; financial responsibility for running schools (except for primary schools with fewer than 200 pupils) is largely devolved to governors, and therefore heads. The notion appears to have emanated from experimentation in Cambridgeshire. It demands of headteachers an expertise in management and in finance which few have or could be expected to have. In the independent sector bursars with the status of at least deputy head have customarily managed school finances. In Coopers and Lybrand Associates' report (1988) on the local financial management of schools they stated:

> The operation of LMS will remove from LEAS the detailed control of most school activities. It will replace that control with a clearer responsibility for setting objectives for schools and for managing the school system as a whole.

Experience has indicated that there are services such as careers guidance which are best provided on an area basis and it is reassuring that LEAS will be allowed to continue to offer such support services. Another provision of the Act has led to predictions of serious imbalance in school rolls, namely 'open enrolment'. The number of pupils admitted to schools will essentially be determined by demand up to their physical capacity instead of what has been termed the 'standard number', usually the number admitted in 1979–80. Local authority staff believe that this will nullify much of their educational planning.

Most controversial of all perhaps are the proposals under which school governing bodies may 'opt out' from local authority control after publishing plans for all interested parties to comment upon. The original wording of the Bill provided for an application for 'grant-maintained status' to be made if parents showed their approval by a simple majority of those voting in a secret postal ballot. The Lords introduced a requirement that a majority of all the parents at the school had to vote in favour of an application. To meet the concern that a small group of parents could seek to determine the future of a school without the consequences being fully appreciated by all parents, the Government responded with amendments introducing a new dual-ballot arrangement. If fewer than 50 per cent of parents vote in a first ballot then a second ballot must be held within fourteen days. Each ballot will be determined by a simple majority and the second ballot, if required, will be conclusive irrespective of turnout. 'Opting out' will create grant-maintained schools which will receive their running costs from the DES through the LEA as well as 100 per cent capital grants directly from the DES. *The Times Educational Supplement* of 2 October 1987 reported: 'Overwhelming condemnation of the government proposals to allow schools to apply to opt out of local authority control has come from education officers, teachers, local government and all the larger organisations of parents.' But the Government in its consultation paper stated that the 'opting-out' proposals will 'add a new and powerful dimension to the ability of parents to exercise choice within the publicly provided sector of education' and should 'enhance the prospect of improving educational standards in all schools'. As the Secretary of State had put it in his January 1987 speech, 'Grant-maintained schools will be a threat to the complacent and to the second-best.' A

Government-backed but independent and privately funded Grant Maintained Schools Trust was established in July 1988 to advise on the scheme.

The Act provides for the establishment of another new form of school: city technological colleges. The plan was outlined at the Conservative Party Conference at Blackpool in October 1986 when it was stated that the colleges were:

> to provide a broadly based secondary education with a strong technological element, thereby offering a wider choice of secondary school to parents in certain cities and a surer preparation for adult and working life to their children.
>
> (DES press release: *City Technology Colleges*)

Each CTC is planned to serve a catchment area which will permit the choice of 750–1,000 pupils from a potential 5,000 and to aim at admitting pupils from a full range of ability, a point which has not been widely understood. It is hoped that some twenty CTCs may exist by 1990 as registered independent schools charging no fee but sponsored by local commerce and industry. Kenneth Baker told the National Grammar Schools Association Conference in July 1988: 'The Balfour Act gave LEAs the monopoly to provide free education; we are ending that monopoly.' Interestingly, the Government has yielded to public pressure and accepted that the syllabuses of CTCs should provide for study of the humanities as well as of science and technology. Addressing the British Academy on the role of the humanities in July 1988 the Secretary of State acknowledged: 'Analytical ability, judgement and fluency of communication are highly prized by employers; and not only among those employers who have traditionally recruited from among arts graduates.'

The national curriculum

The first clauses of the Act embody the provisions for a national curriculum for pupils in maintained schools from 5 to 16 and for the administration of nationally prescribed tests at 7, 11, 14 and 16, which will be externally moderated and on which a Task Group on Assessment and Testing has been established to advise the Secretary of State. The national curriculum consists of core subjects — mathematics, English and science and Welsh in Welsh-speaking schools — and of foundation subjects (history, geography, technology, music, art and physical education and a modern language for those over 11). It will be taught in all maintained primary, secondary and special schools, though 'statemented' children may be excused from some foundation subjects. Religious education, at first excluded from being listed, was placed on a special footing during the passage of the Bill in deference to the strength of representations made. The amount of time to be spent on each subject will not be prescribed but the DES will offer guidance. Subject working groups will advise the Secretary of State on the content and teaching of their subjects; advice will also come from a statutory National Curriculum Council and School Examinations and Assessment Council. The purpose of the national curriculum, Kenneth Baker stressed to the North of England Conference in January 1988, is educational:

> The provisions in the Bill are not designed to enhance the powers of the holder of my office. They are designed to enhance the life chances of the young ... it is surely right that Parliament should take the principal decisions about what the national curriculum should consist of.

Many educationalists deplore the manner in which the curriculum development of the last two decades and more, which has favoured integration of subject areas rather than the teaching of discrete subjects, has been ignored in the national curriculum proposals. There is no doubt, however, that there is much support among parents for these plans. As Richard Jameson, formerly Under Secretary for Finance and Accountant General at the DES, has put it:

> Parents, from Hexham to Helston, want to be sure that their children spend more of their school life on the fundamentals of education, regardless of where they live or of the latest whims of an education committee or local authority adviser. (Jameson, 1988, p. 5)

Equally, many parents, if the opinion polls are anything to go by, welcome the powers given to the Secretary of State by clause 4 to specify attainment targets, programmes of study and assessment

91

arrangements, as well as the indications of increased parental power. In introducing the Bill in the House of Commons, Kenneth Baker commented that it 'will galvanize parental involvement in schools' — no less. The proposals for testing are a case in point. As *The Times* put it on 14 January 1988:

> The system will enable teachers and parents to identify from the age of seven those who need help because they are falling behind and those who need help to stay ahead. Never again will teachers be able to fob off parents who want to know how their children are doing with a jumble of jargon and anodyne assurances.

Whether the tests are, as the consultative paper claimed, 'a proven and essential way towards raising standards of achievement' is another matter entirely. The Task Group on Assessment and Testing in its report published in January 1988 asked that the national assessment system should be criterion-referenced and primarily formative and that gradings should be moderated to secure comparable standards and to ensure pupils' progression. It drew attention to the need for considerably increased resources through Education Support Grants and through training grants for teachers, a point which has been emphasized in its supplementary reports.

The debate on the Education Act 1988

The proposals of the Act have been summarized by Kenneth Baker in three words: standards, freedom and choice. On another occasion, the Secretary of State punned that the Education Reform Act will be the beginning of a new ERA. The Act has been subjected to detailed and at times fierce criticism. To be fair, the Government has responded to this with a considerable number of amendments. From its introduction into the House of Commons in November 1987 to its passage in July 1988 the Act grew from 147 clauses to 238 and 13 schedules. It occupied 220 hours of debate in the Commons and 154 in the Lords. It was not at first proposed that religious education should have the status of a core subject but in the event the Government agreed to amend the Bill to ensure that RE is statutorily defined as part of the basic curriculum to be provided for all pupils by all maintained schools and that it takes its place before core and foundation subjects. However, parents still have the right to withdraw children from RE and collective worship. As the result of a Lords amendment, religious education and school assemblies will in future have to have a predominantly Christian character although pupils from other religions will of course be allowed their own acts of worship.

The Government proved unrelenting on another aspect of its proposals, however, the abolition of the largest English education authority, the Inner London Education Authority. This is going ahead despite numerous representations to the contrary and despite a constant cry from governmental spokesmen that local authorities have a crucial role to play in the development of education. For example, Kenneth Baker told the Council of Local Education Authorities on 15 July 1988:

> The system as it develops will be much more decentralised. But it will be financed by local government; organised by local government; it will be monitored and professionally supported by local government; and it will be accountable to local government. A decentralised system would require more leadership, not less.
>
> (DES *News*, 15 July 1988)

Some of the opposition to the Reform Act has come from rather unexpected quarters. Lord Joseph, as he has become, tried unsuccessfully to amend the Bill to remove the compulsory national curriculum on the grounds that it was over-prescriptive and imposed a straitjacket on the profession. Admittedly, he had stated in his speech (*Why teach history?*) to the Historical Association on 10 February 1984: 'It is not part of the responsibilities of the holder of my office to put forward a single model curriculum for all our schools.' Lord Callaghan, the former Labour Prime Minister, condemned the opting-out provisions as socially divisive and held that it would only be a matter of time before grant-maintained schools won the right to charge fees. The National Foundation for Educational Research

93

divisive =
cause disagreement

has called for the DES and local authorities to take urgent steps to enrol and train responsible people to undertake the new role of school governors and the Audit Commission has drawn attention to the need to plan the changeover in financial management (both July 1988). What has become clear is that if Keith Joseph was a visionary, Kenneth Baker was a committed realist; as he told assembled directors of business and industry in March 1988:

> If you look at a 16-year-old German boy or girl at their technical schools, they take an examination that includes the German language, mathematics, a foreign language, technology plus two other subjects. Nine out of ten pass. The equivalent examination in Britain is the old CSE Grade 4. And only four out of ten of our children pass in a similar range of subjects. That's a huge disparity.
>
> (*Director*, March 1988, p. 43)

Certainly, no one can deny that it is shaming that nearly 40 per cent of children have left British schools in the last quarter of a century or more after eleven years of full-time education with little to show for it. It is also a matter for serious concern that the most up-to-date statistics available about school leavers' qualifications (for 1985–6) show that the proportions with at least one A level, with 5 or more higher grade (A–C) O levels, and with one O level or CSE equivalent have been virtually unchanged since 1983.

The Higginson Report

There is, however, a limit to the current government's radicalism in education. There was much hope in the world of education that the committee chaired by Dr Gordon Higginson, Vice-Chancellor of Southampton, would succeed in reforming the A-level examination. For more than a couple of decades, it has been widely recognized that A levels tend to be too narrow and specialist and numerous proposals have been made for their broadening, including the proposal that they should include major and minor subjects and that the International Baccalaureate should be adopted. In 1986 the Government put forward AS levels as a

94

means of widening the base of studies, but in summer 1988 rejected the Higginson Committee's recommendation of five 'leaner, tougher' subjects rather than the traditional three subjects, despite widespread support in industry and commerce, and despite the fact that the recommended course was in line with the GCSE examinations from which most of the students would be proceeding, in stressing the importance of the process as well as the content of learning. Some A-level examinations have indeed incorporated the precepts of GCSE, for example the examination for the 16 to 19 Geography Project, but most have continued to reward knowledge of facts. The Government's decision will put the emphasis on broadening sixth form studies by means of AS levels — and delay the reform of A levels by perhaps a decade.

Further and higher education

Particularly strong criticism has been made of the Education Reform Act's provisions relating to the universities, which have been seen as giving central government massive new powers of detailed intervention in university internal affairs, threatening their autonomy and the principle of academic freedom. Certainly, University Commissioners are appointed under the Act to amend where necessary the statutes of universities to remove academic tenure from newly appointed or promoted staff as from 20 November 1987. Again, the University Grants Committee is to be replaced by the Universities Funding Council. Lord Annan, the former Vice-Chancellor of London, wrote in a letter to *The Times* of 3 February 1988 that 'when a convention becomes a fiction, it is better to tell the truth'. He was referring to the fact that from the time of the Robbins Report of 1963 the UGC had become increasingly the arm of the government, reluctantly operating a system of norms and other administrative devices that diminish university autonomy. After the oil crisis of 1973 and the collapse of the quinquennial system of funding, he argued, the UGC spent more time advising universities than advising the government. The government would argue, as

Robert Jackson, Parliamentary Under-Secretary of State, DES, did in *The Times* on 23 January 1988, that the replacement of the UGC by the UFC represents a strengthening of the constitutional safeguards for university autonomy: 'Instead of advising the Secretary of State on the allocation of funds, it will have the responsibility for allocating those funds itself directly.'

Lord Annan believes that the expansion of higher education 'has got wrecked on parity of esteem' not only between universities and polytechnics but also between universities, and that it is going to be essential for the UFC to give preferential funding to a dozen or so — a Baker's dozen? — of the university institutions in Britain. Lord Croham's committee on the UGC had reported in February 1987 that a reform was necessary to ensure that proper weight be given to judgements about 'the public interest, about wider economic and social questions, about prospective developments in industry and commerce, and about issues of finance and management' (DES, 1987, para. 3.10). Because ultimately the Secretary of State is responsible to Parliament, paragraph 5.9 of the report recommended a reserve power, as had been provided in respect of the research councils, 'to issue directions to the Council, if need be'. Vice-Chancellors have not in general felt encouraged by the comparison with research councils. Two ex-chairmen of the Science and Engineering Research Council have asserted publicly that there have indeed been directions from the Secretary of State. Total expenditure on research by the UGC and the Research Councils increased from £1,185 million in 1979–80 to £1,287 million in 1987–8, an average annual increase of only one per cent — in other words, a real cut. The Government yielded to pressure so to amend the Bill that the Council, and not the Secretary of State, could attach conditions to influence the allocation of funds between individual institutions.

The polytechnics have felt happier with the developments under the Reform Act. The Polytechnics and Colleges Funding Council parallels the UFC and thus offers both release from local authority control and promise of equality with the university sector; academic tenure has never applied to polytechnics anyway. The White Paper, *Higher Education — Meeting the Challenge* (April 1987), contained a significant comment on the 'efficiency' of polytechnics and colleges of higher education:

> The productivity of higher education as a whole has increased greatly since 1979. Average unit costs are estimated to have fallen in real terms between 1980–81 and 1986–87: by 5 per cent in universities, by 15 per cent in polytechnics and local authority colleges and about 15 per cent in voluntary and other grant aided colleges in England ... The Government ... is committed to achieving the further gains in value for money that will be needed, particularly if access to higher education is to be widened in the future. (paras 3.3, 3.4)

Colleges of further and higher education have commonly been strongly supported by their local authorities and communities; understandably, they have felt more threatened by change. As Minister of State, Lady Hooper told the Industrial Society conference on the report of the Joint Efficiency Study on non-advanced further education in November 1987:

> Effectiveness and efficiency are the key themes of the Government's proposals for the reform of further education ... We believe that it would be an improvement if governing bodies were limited to a sensible size, if they were guaranteed a proper measure of independence, and if those who most nearly represent the consumer were given a stronger voice. (DES *News*, 3 November 1987)

Financial independence from local authorities will place enormous responsibilities on staff and governors, responsibilities which will require training. For colleges with more than 200 full-time-equivalent students, the local education authority will be required by law to calculate the college's total resources for that given year, and the board of governors will determine how this sum should best be spent. Moreover, colleges will be allowed to retain income obtained from their own initiatives rather than have it clawed back by the authority. These provisions will apply to a wide range of colleges, not just to those who may employ hundreds of staff and expend many millions of pounds a year but also to the smaller sixth form or tertiary colleges which have been created in an age of falling secondary rolls, and to music, drama and art colleges.

The provisions in the Reform Act for further and higher education are all of a piece with the Government's general thinking on education. As Kenneth Baker put it in his speech to the North of England Education Conference in January 1988:

> The Government has no wish to interfere in the running of the universities and polytechnics and colleges. Our purpose is to clarify their objectives, require them to give an account of their stewardship to their customers and their cash providers and allow the Vice-Chancellors and Principals to manage properly the institutions for which they have responsibility.

It can only be for the good that the 'binary system' of separate development for universities on the one hand and the public sector institutions of higher education on the other should be brought to an end by the Reform Act, and that courses in further and higher education in polytechnics and colleges should no longer require the Secretary of State's approval. Equally, the public sector could only welcome the disbandment of the National Advisory Board for local authority higher education which had been established early on in the Thatcher government's period of office 'to contribute to a co-ordinated approach to provision, as necessary in relevant academic fields, between the local authority, grant-aided and university sectors of higher education and between the provision in England and that in other countries of the United Kingdom'.

NAB proved, from central government's viewpoint, a poor instrument for rationalization of courses and institutions; the majority of provider interests on the Board precluded enthusiasm for closures and meant that student access tended to be a first priority. NAB and UGC have produced a series of transbinary scrutinies of particular subject areas in accordance with the Board's terms of reference. The Board, as the instrument of cuts in funding for the public sector with access to HMI reports, has incurred a certain opprobrium among the colleges in a way that the Council for National Academic Awards which has validated public sector courses since 1964 has not. There has been a general agreement with the opinion expressed by the CNAA itself:

> The Council is convinced that the discipline involved in preparing and documenting a proposal for the approval or reapproval of a course of study is extremely valuable to the College submitting it ... this discipline contributes to clarifying the aims and objectives of the course and demands the formation of an academic team which identifies itself strongly with the course.
>
> (CNAA, 1974, Appendix 2, para. 5)

The future clearly lies in a larger measure of co-operation between all higher education institutions. One such development has been the creation since 1987 of regional technology centres, which it is hoped will play a crucial role 'in regenerating British industry through the introduction of new technologies supported by the research and training expertise of higher education' (DES *News*, 7 May 1987). Another is the Enterprise in Higher Education scheme launched in 1987 by the Manpower Services Commission to develop more enterprising graduates by making them more aware of the needs of industry and commerce by giving

Teac

All edu   hing staff
and se   adequacy
of sup   atics and
craft,   itation of
the na   e undertaken   lic sector
and, fr   . In 1982
HMI pu   ch stated
that n   showed
deficie   acquired
in trair   ), set out
the req   uncil for
the Accreditation of Teacher Education was established to advise

the Secretaries of State for Education and Science and for Wales on the approval of training courses. Membership of the Council was distinguished by a noticeable dearth of teacher trainers, but paragraph 9 of DES Circular 3/84 stated:

> A course will be considered for approval only if it has the support of a local committee on which the training institution, the local education authorities in the area, local practising school teachers and individuals from outside the education service are all represented.

It was hoped that the work of these local committees would strengthen the links between a training institution, schools and the community; and facilitate developments such as allowing practising teachers to participate in the selection, training, supervision and assessment of students; giving opportunities for teacher training staff to refresh their knowledge and experience of classroom teaching; and ensuring that students' work with classes, small groups and individual pupils relates closely to their studies. The prescriptive accreditation of teacher training courses parallels the direct central control of the school curriculum and has not helped to raise the quality of teacher training. Rather it has undermined the morale of those engaged in this fundamental area. The best practice in teacher training has always incorporated the prescribed principles in any case. Teacher trainers are accustomed to accommodating change. As Professor Alec Ross has written:

> In the organisation and management of education there is no point of rest; this applies *a fortiori* to teacher education in which demography, government policy, financial implications and changes in educational philosophy all play an important part.
>
> (UCET, 1987, p. 29)

In-service education of teachers has come to be of crucial importance in an era of change. Teachers used to attend external courses of their choice; it was the consensus of informed opinion that the profession as a whole would benefit as a result. After the James Report of 1972, a new philosophy was mooted which has been referred to as 'a deficit model' of in-service training based on school and individual teachers' needs. Since 1983 there have been several moves by central government to encourage more spending by local authorities on in-service training and in particular on school-focused in-service training, culminating in Circular 6/86, *Grant Related In-Service Training* (GRIST). The main objectives of the new arrangements are to promote the professional development of teachers and to establish a systematic planning of in-service training by the use of education support grants, a process which clearly facilitates central control.

At the same time, a DES consultation document, *Qualified Teacher Status* (May 1988) has made it clear that the Government wishes to encourage re-entrants to teaching, such as married women returners, and new entrants who would have the opportunity to obtain qualified teacher status by means other than an initial teacher training course. These might be 'mature entrants making a career change for whom a period of full-time study would be a disincentive to recruitment as well as overseas-trained teachers. Such individuals have a potentially valuable contribution to make to the schools' (DES, 1988, p. 2). They would be known as licensed teachers (shades of pupil teachers?). No wonder that Professor Brian Simon warned in 1985, 'The historical record clearly shows that there is nothing inevitable about education advance' (Simon, 1985, p. 52).

Bibliography

Armytage, W.H.G. (1951), *A.J. Mundella: The Liberal Background of the Labour Movement, 1825–1897*, London, Macmillan.

Armytage, W.H.G. (1970), *Four Hundred Years of English Education*, Cambridge, Cambridge University Press.

Barker, R. (1972), *Education and Politics 1900–51: A Study of the Labour Party*, London, Oxford University Press.

Barlow Report (1946), *See* Committee appointed by Lord President of Council.

Barnes, A. (1977), 'Decision-making on the curriculum in Britain', in R. Glatter (ed.), *Control of the Curriculum*, London, University of London, Institute of Education.

Bennett, N. et al. (1976), *Teaching Styles and Pupil Progress*, London, Open Books.

Bernbaum, G. (ed.)(1979), *Schooling in Decline*, London, Macmillan.

Board of Education (1938), *Report of the Consultative Committee on Secondary Education with Special Reference to Grammar Schools and Technical High Schools* (Spens Report) London, HMSO.

Board of Education (1941), *Education after the War* (Green Book), London, HMSO.

Board of Education (1943), *Educational Reconstruction* (White Paper), London, HMSO.

Board of Education (1944a), *Report of a Committeee appointed by the President of the Board of Education to Consider the Supply, Recruitment and Training of Teachers and Youth Leaders* (McNair Report), London, HMSO.

Board of Education (1944b), *The Public Schools and the General Educational System* (Fleming Report), London, HMSO.

Booth, C. (1902), *Life and Labour of the People of London*, London, Macmillan.

Booth, C. (1987), 'Central government and higher education planning 1965–1986', *History of Education Quarterly*, 4, (I), pp. 57–72.

Bridges, Edward, later Lord (1950), *Portrait of a Profession*, London, Cambridge University Press.

Bruner, Jerome (1986), *Actual Minds, Possible Worlds*, London, Harvard University Press.

Bullock Report (1975), *See* DES.

Butler, R.A. (1982), *The Art of the Possible*, London, Hamish Hamilton (First published 1971).

Clarke, Sir Fred (1940), *Education and Social Change: An English Interpretation*, London, Sheldon Press.

Committee appointed by the Lord President of the Council (1946) *Scientific Manpower* (Barlow Report), London, HMSO.

Commonwealth Immigrants Advisory Council (CIAC) (1964) *Second Report*, London, Oxford University Press.

Community Relations Council (1976), *Funding Multiracial Education: A National Strategy*, London, CRC.

Coopers and Lybrand (1985), *National Data Study*, London, Committee of Vice Chancellors and Principals.

Council for National Academic Awards (1974), *Regulations and Conditions for the Award of the Council's First Degrees*, London, CNAA.

Council of Europe (1973), *Permanent Education: The Basis and the Essentials*, Strasbourg, Council for Cultural Co-operation.

Cox, C.B. and Boyson, Rhodes (1975), *Black Paper*, London, Dent.

Croham Report (1987), *See* DES.

Crosland, A. (1975), *Social Democracy in Europe*, London, Fabian Society.

Crowther Report (1959), *See* Ministry of Education.

Cruickshank, Marjorie (1963), *Church and State in English Education*, London, Macmillan.

Dean, J. and Choppin, B. (1977), *Educational Provision 16–19*, Windsor, National Foundation for Educational Research (NFER).

Dent, H.C. (1969a), *The Education Act 1944*, London, University of London Press.

Dent, H.C. (1969b), *The Educational Systems of England and Wales*, London, University of London Press.

Department of Education and Science (DES) (1966), *The Government Colleges of Education* (Weaver Report), London, HMSO.

DES (1966), *A Plan for Polytechnics* (White Paper), London, HMSO.

DES (1967), *Report of the Central Advisory Council for Education (England): Children and Their Primary Schools* (Plowden Report), London, HMSO.

DES (1972a), *Teacher Education and Training* (James Report), London, HMSO.

DES (1972b), *A Framework for Expansion*, (White Paper), London, HMSO.

103

DES (1972c), *Open Plan Primary Schools*, London, HMSO.

DES (1973), *Adult Education: A Plan for Development* (Russell Report), London, HMSO.

DES (1975), *A Language for Life: Report of the Committee of Inquiry* (Bullock Report), London, HMSO.

DES (1977), *Education in Schools* (Cmnd 6869), London, HMSO.

DES (1977a), *Education in Schools: A Consultative Document* (Green Paper), London, HMSO.

DES (1977b), *A New Partnership for Our Schools* (Taylor Report), London, HMSO.

DES (1978), *Primary Education in England (A Survey by HMI)*, London, HMSO.

DES (1979), *Report on 14/77 Review*, London, HMSO.

DES (1980), *A Framework for the School Curriculum*, London, HMSO.

DES (1981), *The School Curriculum*, London, HMSO.

DES (1983a), *Curriculum 11–16. Towards a Statement of Entitlement, Curriculum Reappraisal in Action*, London, HMSO.

DES (1983b), *9 to 13 Middle Schools*, London, HMSO.

DES (1983c), *Training for Jobs* (White Paper), London, HMSO.

DES (1985a), *Better Schools*, London, HMSO.

DES (1985b), *The Development of Higher Education into the 1990s* (Cmnd 9524).

DES (1987a), *Review of the University Grants Committee* (Croham Report), London, HMSO.

DES (1987b), *Higher Education: Meeting the Challenge* (White Paper), London, HMSO.

DES (1988), *Qualified Teacher Status: Consultation Document*, London, HMSO.

Douglas, J.W.B. (1964), *The Home and the School*, London, MacGibbon & Kee.

Dunford, J.R. (1987), *The Association of Education Committees and School Building Policy in England and Wales, 1944–64*, Leeds, Museum of the History of Education, University of Leeds.

Easen, P. (ed.) (1975), *Making School-centred Inset Work*, London, Croom Helm for the Open University.

Education Act 1944, London, HMSO.

Fenwick, I.G.K. and McBride, P. (1981), *The Government of Education*, Oxford, Robertson.

Fleming Report (1944), *See* Board of Education.

Floud, Jean, Halsey, A.H. and Anderson, C.A. (eds) (1961), *Education, Economy and Society*, Collier-Macmillan.

Fowler, W.S. (1988), *Towards the National Curriculum: Discussion and Control in the English Educational System 1965–88*, London, Kogan Page.

Glennerster, H. and Pryke, R. (1964), *The Public Schools*, London, Fabian Society.

Gosden, P.H.J.H. (1976), *Education in the Second World War*, London, Methuen.

Gosden, P.H.J.H. (1981), 'Twentieth-century archives of education as sources for the study of educational policy and administration', *Archives*, 15 (66), pp. 86–95.

Hadow, Sir W.H. (1926), *Report of the Consultative Committee: The Education of the Adolescent*, London, HMSO.

Hadow, Sir W.H. (1931), *Report of the Consultative Committee on the Primary School*, London, HMSO.

Hall, J.R. (1912), *The Armstrong Schools Elswick: Some Reminiscences and Impressions*, Newcastle, privately printed.

Halsey, A.H. (1978), *Change in British Society*, London, Oxford University Press.

Hiro, D. (1971), *Black Britain, White Britain*, London, Eyre & Spottiswoode.

Her Majesty's Inspectorate of Schools (HMI) (1977), *Curriculum 11–16*, London, HMSO.

HMI (1980), *A View of the Curriculum* (HMI Matters for Discussion no. 11), London, HMSO.

HMI (1982), *Education 5–9: An Illustrated Study by HMI*, London, HMSO.

HMI (1985), *The Curriculum from 5–16* (Curriculum Matters no. 2), London, HMSO.

James Report (1972), *See* DES.

James, P.H. (1980), *The Reorganization of Secondary Education*, Slough, National Foundation for Educational Research.

Jameson, R. (1988), 'The Baker Bill: An outside view', *Report*, 10 (5), pp. 4–5.

Jamieson, I., Miller, A. and Watts, A.G. (1988), *Mirrors at Work: Work Simulations in Schools*, Lewes, E. Sussex, Falmer Press.

Jeffereys, Kevin (1984), 'R.A. Butler, the Board of Education and the 1944 Education Act', *History*, 69 (227), pp. 415–31.

Kekewich, Sir George (1920), *The Education Department and After*, London, Constable.

Kogan, M. (1971), *The Politics of Education*, Harmondsworth, Penguin.

Kogan, M. (1975), *Educational Policy-Making*, London, Allen & Unwin.

Lambert, R. (1975), *The Chance of a Lifetime? A Study of Boys' and Co-educational Boarding Schools in England and Wales*, London, Weidenfeld & Nicolson.

Lauglo, J. and McLean, M. (eds) (1985), *The Control of Education*, London, Heinemann.

Lawton, D. (1984), *The Tightening Grip: Growth of Central Control of the*

School Curriculum, (Bedford Way Papers 21) London, University of London, Institute of Education.

Lowndes, G.A.N. (1969), *The Silent Social Revolution: An Account of the Expansion of Public Education in England and Wales 1895–1965*, London, Oxford University Press (2nd ed.).

Maclure, J.S. (1971), *Educational Documents: England and Wales 1816–1968*, London, Methuen.

Maclure, J.S. (1985), 'Forty years on', *British Journal of Educational Studies*, 33, (2), pp. 117–34.

McNair Report (1944), *See* Board of Education.

McPherson, A. and Raab, C.D. (1988), *Governing Education: A Sociology of Policy since 1945*, Edinburgh, Edinburgh University Press.

Magnus, P. (1910), *Educational Aims and Efforts 1880–1910*, London, Longmans, Green.

Marshall, S. (1963), *An Experiment in Education*, Cambridge, Cambridge University Press.

Middleton, N. with Weitzman, S. (1976), *A Place for Everyone: A History of State Education from the End of the 18th Century to the 1970s*, London, Victor Gollancz.

Ministry of Education (1944), *Standard Construction for Schools*, London, HMSO.

Ministry of Education (1947), *The New Secondary Education*, Pamphlet no. 9, London, HMSO.

Ministry of Education (1954), *Early Leaving. Report of the Central Advisory Council for Education (England)*, London, HMSO.

Ministry of Education (1956), *Technical Education* (White Paper), London, HMSO.

Ministry of Education (1957), *Training of Teachers*, Pamphlet no. 34, London, HMSO.

Ministry of Education (1959), *15 to 18. Report of the Central Advisory Council for Education (England)*, (Crowther Report), London, HMSO.

Ministry of Education (1963a), *Higher Education. Report of the Committee appointed by the Prime Minister under the Chairmanship of Lord Robbins 1961–3*, (Robbins Report), London, HMSO.

Ministry of Education (1963b), *Half Our Future. Report of the Central Advisory Council for Education (England)*, (Newsom Report), London, HMSO.

Morgan, K. (1984), *Labour in Power 1945–1951*, London, Oxford University Press.

Newsom Report (1963), *See* Ministry of Education.

Niblett, W.R. et al. (1975), *The University Connection*, Slough, National Foundation for Educational Research (NFER).

OECD (1975), *Educational Development Strategy in England and Wales*, Paris: Organization for Economic and Cultural Development (OECD).

Open University (1979), *Educational Studies: A Second Level Course, E222 The Control of Education in Britain*, especially Unit 12 'The Colleges and Schools: Provision for the 16–19-year-olds', Milton Keynes, Open University Press.

Parsons, C. (1978), *Schools in an Urban Community: A Study of Carbrook, 1870–1965*, London, Routledge & Kegan Paul.

Percy, Lord Eustace (1945), *Higher Technical Education*. Report of a special committee appointed by the Ministry of Education, London, HMSO.

Pile, Sir William D. (1979), *The Department of Education and Science*, London, Allen & Unwin.

Plowden Report (1969), *See* DES.

Pring, R. (1985), 'In defence of TVEI', *Forum*, 28, (1), pp. 4–17.

Public Schools Commission (1968), *First Report*, London, HMSO.

Quicke, John (1988), 'The "New Right" and Education', *British Journal of Education Studies*, (1), pp. 5–20.

Redcliffe-Maud Report (1969), *See* Royal Commission.

Regan, D.E. (1977), *Local Government and Education*, London, Allen & Unwin.

Report (1834), *Report of the Parliamentary Committee on the State of Education (1834)*, London, HMSO.

Report (1861), *Report of the Commissioners Appointed to Inquire into the State of Popular Education in England* (Newcastle Commission), London, HMSO.

Report (1864), *Report of the Commissioners Appointed to Inquire into the Revenues and Management of Certain Schools and the Studies Pursued and Instruction Given Therein* (Clarendon Commission) First Part, General Report, London, HMSO.

Rich, E.E. (1970), *The Education Act, 1870: A Study of Public Opinion*, Harlow, Longman.

Richmond, W.K. (1978), *Education in Britain since 1944: A Personal Retrospect*, London, Methuen.

Robbins Report (1963), *See* Ministry of Education.

Royal Commission (1969), *Royal Commission on Local Government in England Report* (Redcliffe-Maud Report), London, HMSO.

Runciman, J. (1887), *Schools and Scholars*, London, Chatto & Windus.

Russell Report (1973), *See* Department of Education and Science.

Salter, B. and Tapper, T. (1982), *Education Policy and the State: Theory and Practice of Educational Change*, London, Grant McIntyre.

Sampson, G. (1926), *English for the English: A Chapter on National Education*, Cambridge, Cambridge University Press (First edition 1921).

Schools Council (1975), *The Whole Curriculum 13–16* (Working Paper 53), London, Evans/Methuen.

Short, Edward, later Lord Glenamara (1968–9), *Evidence to Select*

Committee on Education and Science 1968–9.

Silver, H. (1980), *Education and the Social Condition*, London, Methuen.

Simon, B. (1985), *Does Education Matter?* London, Lawrence & Wishart.

Simon, B. (1986), 'The 1944 Education Act: A Conservative measure?' *History of Education*, 15 (1), pp. 31–43.

Smith, W.O. Lester (1942), *To Whom Do the Schools Belong? An Introduction to the Study of School Government*, Oxford, Blackwell.

Spens Report (1938), *See* Board of Education.

Sullivan, F.B. (1980), *Lord Butler: The 1944 Act in Retrospect*, London, Open University Press.

Tawney, R.H. (ed.) (1922), *Secondary Education for All*. London, Labour Party Education Advisory Committee.

Tawney, R.H. (1964, 5th ed.) *Equality, The Halley Stewart Lectures for 1929*, London, Allen & Unwin (First published 1931).

Thompson, F.M.L. (1981), 'Social control in Victorian Britain', *Economic History Review*, 2nd series, 34, (2), pp. 189–208.

Titmuss, R.M. (1950), *Problems of Social Policy*, London, Longman.

Universities Council for the Education of Teachers (1973), *The Inservice Education and Training of Teachers*, London, UCET.

Universities Council for the Education of Teachers (1987), *The Universities Council for the Education of Teachers 1966–1987: Twenty-one Years of Endeavour*, London, UCET.

University Grants Committee (1976), *Annual Survey, Academic Year 1974–75*, London, HMSO.

Vaizey, John, later Lord (1963), *The Control of Education*, London, Faber & Faber.

Wallace, R.G. (1981), 'The origins and authorship of the 1944 Education Act', *History of Education*, 10, (4), pp. 283–90.

Watts, A.G. (1983), *Education, Unemployment and the Future of Work*, Milton Keynes, Open University Press.

Weaver Report (1966), *See* Department of Education and Science.

Weaver, Sir Toby (1976), *Unity and Diversity in Education*.

Worsley, T.C. (1940), *Barbarians and Philistines: Democracy and the Public Schools*, London, Hale.

Wyatt, H. (1985), 'TVEI and all that', *Forum*, 27 (3), pp. 72–4.

Further reading

The most readable general history of English education remains John Lawson and Harold Silver, *A Social History of Education in England* (Methuen, 1973). The economic background for the nineteenth and early twentieth centuries is well reviewed in Eric Hopkins, *A Social History of the English Working Classes 1815–1945* (Edward Arnold, 1979). J.S. Hurt's *Elementary Schooling and the Working Classes 1860–1918* (Routledge & Kegan Paul, 1979) is balanced by John Roach's *A History of Secondary Education in England 1800–1870* (Longman, 1986), which is expected to be followed by a further volume. For public school education, see J. R. de S. Honey, *Tom Brown's Universe* (Millington, 1977). For an outline of teacher training, see H.C. Dent, *The Training of Teachers in England and Wales 1800–1975* (Hodder & Stoughton, 1977). For universities, see W.H.G. Armytage, *Civic Universities: Aspects of a British Tradition* (Benn, 1955) and J.M. Sanderson, *The Universities in the Nineteenth Century* (Routledge & Kegan Paul, 1975) and *The Universities and British Industry 1850–1970* (Routledge & Kegan Paul, 1972). Brian Simon has published a three-volume *tour de force*, *Studies in the History of Education vol. 1: The Two Nations and the Educational Structure, 1780–1870; vol. 2: Education and the Labour Movement, 1870–1920; vol. 3: The Politics of Educational Reform, 1920–1940* (Lawrence & Wishart, 1960, revised 1974, 1965, 1974 respectively) and plans a fourth volume covering 1940–80. Roy Lowe has recently produced *Education in the Post-War Years: A Social History* which deals with the period 1945–64 (Routledge, 1988) and plans a further volume. Harold Silver's *Education and the Social Condition* (Methuen, 1980) is a stimulating general discussion; Stewart Ranson and John Tomlinson, *The Changing Government of Local Education* (Allen & Unwin for the Institute of Local Government Studies, 1986), a more specific study. G.R. Barrell and J.A. Partington, *Teachers and the Law* (Methuen, 6th ed., 1985) is an invaluable book of reference as is J. Stuart Maclure, *Educational Documents England and Wales 1816–Present Day* (Methuen, 5th ed., 1985). *The National Curriculum*, Bedford Way Papers 33 (University of London Institute of Education, 1988) is a collection of papers on diverse aspects of this contentious subject edited by Denis Lawton and Clyde Chitty and is well worth reading.

Name index

Subject index